DEWITT COMMUNITY LIBRARY
SHOPPINGTOWN MALL
3649 ERIE BLVD, EAST
DEWITT, NEW YORK 13214

RICHARD ANDERSON

At Last...A **MEMOIR**

From the Golden Years of **M-G-M**
To *The Six Million Dollar Man*
To Today

As Told To
ALAN DOSHNA

RICHARD ANDERSON: AT LAST...A MEMOIR
FROM THE GOLDEN YEARS OF M-G-M
TO THE SIX MILLION DOLLAR MAN TO TODAY

COPYRIGHT 2015 RICHARD ANDERSON AND ALAN DOSHNA

ALL RIGHTS RESERVED.

No part of this book may be reproduced in any form or by any means, electronic, mechanical, digital, photocopying, or recording, except for inclusion of a review, without permission in writing from the publisher.

Published in the USA by:

BEARMANOR MEDIA
P.O. BOX 71426
ALBANY, GEORGIA 31708
www.BearManorMedia.com

ISBN-10: 1-59393-804-7 (alk. paper)
ISBN-13: 978-1-59393-804-8 (alk. paper)

DESIGN AND LAYOUT: VALERIE THOMPSON

TABLE OF CONTENTS

A CURSE AND A BLESSING...1

"YOU OUGHT TO WRITE A BOOK"...7

CHAPTER ONE: RELOCATION...9

CHAPTER TWO: THE M-G-M YEARS: PART ONE...23

CHAPTER THREE: THE M-G-M YEARS: PART TWO...41

CHAPTER FOUR: PATHS OF GLORY, THE FACELESS MAN & ZORRO...63

CHAPTER FIVE: PERRY MASON, THE NIGHT STRANGLER AND "THE LAST FRAME"...81

CHAPTER SIX: "WE HAVE THE TECHNOLOGY."...95

CHAPTER SEVEN: THE POST-"BIONIC" YEARS...111

CHAPTER EIGHT: SOME OLD FAVORITES...117

CHAPTER NINE: ON BEING AN ACTOR...121

CHAPTER TEN: UP CLOSE AND PERSONAL...129

CHAPTER NOTES...141

ACKNOWLEDGMENTS...147

FOR MORE INFORMATION ABOUT RICHARD ANDERSON...149

INDEX...151

THE AUTHORS...157

Photo courtesy of Richard Anderson

To Katharine
– R. A.

To Ma and Don
And to Richard
for your faith in my work
– A. D.

A Curse and a Blessing

As a boy, I loved movies. For some years after we had relocated, my mom had the newspaper from our hometown of Yonkers, NY, delivered to our new home in the upstate Syracuse area. I enjoyed checking out the TV listings to see what scary movies would be playing on "Chiller Theatre" down there on Saturday nights, as such were rare on the channels in our area at the time.

On this one particular weekend when we would be going down to visit friends and relatives, Chiller would be showing the motion picture *Curse of the Faceless Man*. One of the few paperback movie review listings of that time gave out ratings:

Poor: Fair Good: Excellent.

Yes, it was "Excellent."

I immediately recognized the film's charismatic leading man, Richard Anderson, although I couldn't pinpoint exactly where from at that moment: No doubt from watching *The Rifleman* and *The Big Valley* reruns after school, or from seeing *Paths of Glory*, probably the greatest war film ever made, on the afternoon movie (including the horrifying scene where the three innocent soldiers are executed, which made a resounding impression on me).

And the curse of the Faceless Man was this: There was Quintillus Aurelius, the lava man of the film's title: a centuries-old spirit living in the material world, stripped of his identity, his place, his time, and most dearly, the love of his life by a rain of volcanic fire and brimstone. She would move on through the ages in the company of strangers until his one final attempt at physical reunion, and a battle with Richard Anderson for the lady, ending with the surrender of his mortal coil in the waters of the Mediterranean, hopefully to find release, if not peace.

I was overcome by the power of the film, which seemed to offer a portal into its own minimalist universe. It was then and there on that evening somehow, I knew that for better or worse, my future would be involved with the entertainment field.

I soon began to notice the name Richard Anderson in other credits, particularly horror/sci-fi/fantasy films which I was interested in, such as John Frankenheimer's *Seconds* and *Seven Days in May*, as well as Vincent Minnelli's *The Story of Three Loves*, Martin Ritt's *The Long, Hot Summer* and the film that led the way to the Sci-Fi age, the *Star Wars* forerunner *Forbidden Planet*.

And it was only a few years later that *The Six Million Dollar Man* really put Richard's career into high gear in the public eye. And in fact, you will read in these pages that, at an earlier time, a famous star's wife saw him on television and called her husband in to watch this young man doing a comedy scene with a beautiful lady—and agreed to mentor Richard toward a seven-year contract with Metro Goldwyn Mayer.

Even so, I still feel to this day *I* was the one who discovered him on TV that night in Wappingers Falls, and was duly proud of his new success!

Out in California now, my knowledge of this actor's career continued to grow with his Westerns with Clark Gable, William Holden's *Escape From Fort Bravo*, Stewart Granger's costume action drama *Scaramouche*…and always a prize part, on *The Rifleman* which features the dashing Richard Anderson in fine form as cardsharp gambler "Lariat Jones."

But it would not be for a number of years down the road that I would meet this memorable actor at an autograph show at the Hilton Hotel in Burbank, CA. As I approached the table where he was set up, next to that of his Bionic Woman co-star Lindsay Wagner, I was taken aback by his conversation with a couple of his young fans: instead of talking films or about an episode of one of his many TV programs, he came across as more of a person interested in helping, animatedly discussing a popular self help book with them, encouraging one to take a more active role in life.

He quoted Abraham Lincoln (I later learned he is a Lincoln student): "Things work out when you make the best of the way things work out."

All of this while two highly collectible Oscar Goldman action figures waved playfully from the table in front of him.

Clearly, there was more to this man than we were given a chance to see in the many roles we've seen him in.

After agreeing to do an interview with me for a popular movie magazine, I was quickly led to understand why people frequently ask him to write a book about his life. Having decided to call to propose that possibility to him. I soon had a publisher ready to do one: Ben Ohmart of BearManor Media upon hearing that Richard was involved, immediately agreed.

Although a modest and frankly rather private person, Mr. Anderson is openly grateful for and appreciates the interest of fans and/or friends in his life experiences…

He agreed.

It is for this reason that I offered to write this introduction, to at least attempt to put this biography/memoir into an appropriate perspective and framework. This, all leading up to my "hitting the lottery" as it were in having the opportunity to help document the fascinating life of this remarkable man and actor, Richard Anderson.

ALAN DOSHNA

Richard Anderson in *Curse of the Faceless Man* (1958).
Photo courtesy of Richard Anderson.

> **STEVE AUSTIN:**
> **ASTRONAUT**
> **A MAN BARELY ALIVE.**
> **WE CAN REBUILD HIM.**
> **WE CAN MAKE HIM BETTER THAN HE WAS.**
> **BETTER, FASTER, STRONGER.**
> **WE HAVE THE TECHNOLOGY.**

The words were those of Richard Anderson—a familiar and prominent face in theatrical movies and television for decades.

Although he will be forever remembered for his role as Oscar Goldman on *The Six Million Dollar Man* and *The Bionic Woman* television series of the 1970s, the 6'3" motion picture actor began his career much earlier than that.

Richard's early life seemed to provide training, preparation and a foundation for later having contracts with Metro-Goldwyn-Mayer, 20th Century Fox and Universal Studios over a period of forty years. His family's struggle through the Great Depression of the 1930s, the hope instilled in him through his love of movies, life and theatrical experiences qualified him for being at the right place at the right time.

As an actor at MGM from 1949-56, he appeared in twenty four films in his six years under contract. He worked with some of the most celebrated and finest actors and directors of all time in the film business.

Richard's career has spanned Broadway as well as his having made more than eight hundred television appearances, including starring roles in six TV series. These in addition to an amazing number of landmark TV programs ranging from the groundbreaking live broadcast *Playhouse 90* and *Perry Mason*, to *The Wild, Wild West* and *Charlie's Angels*, as well as two years on *Dynasty*.

"Climbing into the saddle," he would co-star in Western films such as *Escape From Fort Bravo* with William Holden, *Across the Wide Missouri* with Clark Gable, with a whole array of television appearances: *The Rifleman, Gunsmoke, The Big Valley* and *Zane Grey Theatre*.

There were also twenty TV movies, among them *The Night Strangler, Murder By Natural Causes, Doctor's Wives, Kane and Abel* and the Hawaiian-based miniseries *Pearl*.

Richard was nominated for an Emmy for his role as Oscar Goldman on *The Bionic Woman* series for the 1976-77 TV season by a POPULAR VOTE, made up of television viewers, prior to changes in Emmy voting rules.

As a producer, five years after the two "Bionic" series were over, Richard reunited the original cast, producing three hugely successful two-hour TV movies, and continues to be involved with the production of television and theatrical motion pictures.

Equally at ease in heroic, action-filled, romantic and colorful roles, the real Richard Anderson is disarmingly engaging to his fans, whom he particularly enjoys meeting at his numerous worldwide personal appearances at conventions.

"You Ought to Write a Book!"

Richard would smile, after answering people's questions about his hundreds of experiences in the film business, working with and later getting to know such luminaries as Clark Gable, Cary Grant, Gary Cooper, Spencer Tracy, Kirk Douglas, Lana Turner, Natalie Wood to name a few. The uniform and inevitable comment:

"Richard, you should write a book about your life!"

He'd always shoot back,

"Why? I'm still living it!"

But what suddenly convinced him to change his mind was an offer from Universal Pictures to co-star in an action series called *The Six Million Dollar Man*.

First of all, it was a great idea based on the book *Cyborg* by Martin Caidin, already known as an outstanding test pilot. The Viet Nam war had created a dark period at this time in American history, which was reflected in the popular movies that were being made. Paul Newman was playing negative roles in films like *Hud*…People were seeing them, having been caught up in the zeitgeist of the times.

After reading *Cyborg*, he felt that if its TV equivalent was written right, it could override the negativity of the Viet Nam war, and this is how:

1. It will bring back the authentic American hero.
2. Movies will have happy endings again
3. Plus, a new medical discovery will be brought to light.

All of which would eventually happen.

On top of it, he was excited about playing the role of Oscar Goldman, who is in charge of the OSI (the Office of Special Investigation)1 in Washington, DC (a Washington, DC, official called the day after the opening show, explaining that there is a real Office of Special Investigation…it was then changed to Office of Scientific Investigation).[1]

When he is told that an Air Force pilot named Steve Austin had crashed his plane, with the loss of an eye, an arm and both legs, Goldman not only orders Dr. Rudy Wells to try a new medical procedure called "bionics" to hopefully replace the body parts, but also to test a new method of warfare. His plan was that, instead of sending armies of troops out to the battle, he would instead have a one-man army to send out on CIA-type missions against enemy forces.

After reading the script, Anderson called his agent immediately and said:

"Look, get me this job even if I have to pay them!"

His agent replied, "They've already made the offer."

And what happened?

For five years, the show was #1 on Sunday night on ABC.

And to add on to this extraordinary story, six months into the show's run, it was reported in the newspapers that a man who had lost his right arm in an accident would medically, through prosthetics, be able to start using it again. This show did more than just entertain.

But enough about the industry…let's hear about the legend that is: Richard Anderson! From the source!

CHAPTER ONE:
RELOCATION

STARTING OVER, FROM THE BEGINNING

There's an old saying regarding financial prosperity: "The first one makes it, the second one spends it, the third one starts all over again."

The Anderson family's successful, first-generation hat manufacturing business called Joseph Anderson and Sons was lost after its founders had all passed away and the Great Depression of 1929 had hit the family hard.

I was born three years prior to that as Richard Norman Anderson in Long Branch, New Jersey on August 8, 1926 to Henry and Olga Anderson. I would be the one to start the cycle over again. This time, thankfully, with a little more staying power.

One morning, while I was sitting in our family's NY east side apartment, where we had since relocated, workers were moving our furniture to lesser accommodations on the west side of New York. I happened to glance out the window and could see a large object outside falling fast. Approaching the window and looking down, I saw that a person had jumped. This perception brought home, in a very dramatic way, the present desperate reality bearing down upon our family and myself.

Richard and Robert Anderson.
Photo courtesy of Richard Anderson

THE 96TH ST. THEATRE

My one joy in those times was going with my brother Bob to the 96th St. Motion Picture Theatre to see matinee showings of movies of the golden era of films, plus WESTERNS…my favorite.

I looked at this world of heroes and happy endings as though it were real—a real, better world that I wanted to be part of. I earnestly, yet mistakenly, believed that the world I saw on the screen was real. Most people went to movies to escape. But I had a bigger plan. I wanted to be an actual part of this better, happier world.

Another drawing point was that I saw an actor in these Westerns who would later become one of the giants of film history; watching him made me decide that I too would become an actor.

He was lean, tall, didn't say much. He was a *minimalist.*

Original expressions, using "body language" to carry the film along.

Seventeen years later, I had just signed my own seven-year contract at Metro and was invited, shortly after, to appear at a film festival in Mexico City. Not long after my arrival I received a call from a friend who said "Come on up. He's here!"

Walked in. There he was: standing, talking on the phone.

He looked great, just like in the movies. Well dressed, had a shirt made in Italy. He had on a short coat, made him look taller.

I was introduced. We talked movies. The actor revealed that when he and his leading lady did their first scene together, he knew right then if the picture would be any good.

I asked "Why?"

The actor mumbled

"*Chemistry.*"

"You know, Richard, when my agent calls about a movie, I'll say no. He calls again, I'll say no. There's only one time, I'll say yes."

"When is that?"

"When I get the GIRL at the END…"

I then asked him another question: "What is the most important thing for a film actor?"

"Good feet."

How right he was. Actors have a *lot* of standing around on the set…waiting until THEY'RE ready to shoot.

"One more question."
He hesitated. "What about?"
"Acting...."
He paused just like he did in the movies...Then:
"Well I, don't know too much about that, but don't ever get caught doing it."
The actor was Gary Cooper.

Heading West

As the depression hit everybody hard, my father bought a used 1932 four-door Buick and announced to our family that we were heading west for a fresh start in life.

So on a bright summer morning in New York City, the whole family met in front of the hotel on the west side to say goodbye to our family. Sitting in the back seat, waving goodbye to them as the car drove off, we headed west.

All along the way, I kept singing (until they finally asked me to shut up): "Oh, Susannah, don't you cry for me, I'm heading to California with a banjo on my knee."

And inside I was thinking "That's where they make the movies."

First "Acting" Experience

Living in Westwood Village, for the next seven years I attended Westwood Grammar School, Emerson Junior High School and University High School.

In a speech class at Emerson Junior High school one day, the teacher asked all classmates to stand up, walk to the head of the class and do a pantomime. When it was my turn, I hesitated and said to myself "What would it be like to smoke your first cigarette?" I faced the class, and in pantomime reached into my shirt pocket, pulled out an imaginary cigarette with my right hand and a book of matches with my left, lit it, inhaled—and started choking!

The place "Went up in smoke!"

Hearing their laughter and feeling the acceptance that I had received from the class, I was given the first confidence in my life and that I just might be able to make it as an actor. The reason I felt that way? I had buck teeth of which I was extremely conscious.

In my senior year at Emerson Junior High School, having never really liked to stand up in front of people I, unannounced and with audacity, signed up on the paper to run for student body president.

When it came time for me to speak, I imitated the most sensational Sunday night news broadcaster in the country:

"Good evening Mr. and Mrs. North and South America and all the ships at sea. This is Walter Winchell. I want to talk to you about one person tonight, a person who should be president of his school. His name is Dick Anderson. The D in Dick does not stand for dictatorship. It stands for democracy."

The audience stood up and applauded.

The opponent's faces turned white.

Although it was announced that I had lost, I had gotten some proof that I had actually won but the three boys wanted to see one of them win and had "made some moves" which gave the vote to my opponent. But I decided that I didn't want to get into it, having learned something about politics and decided right then and there: *Wait till I meet these guys in high school. They're going to get a different ending.* I had a plan...

So, in my first year at University High, I ran for Commissioner of Safety, playing General Douglas McArthur.

The year was 1941. Pearl Harbor had just been bombed. The Japanese were invading The Philippines. In my speech I said:

"I am General McArthur on Bataan, and I and my men are staring at the sky, looking for American planes that never came."

Then McArthur says:

"We need men like Richard Anderson."

I won.

Norma Jean

Part of my job as Commissioner of Safety at University High was to sit at the east gate to make sure that the students had a pass to come to school and leave.

One day, I was eating a 15-cent lunch of egg salad sandwich and my favorite dessert—sherbet.

Sitting there eating raspberry sherbet, the east gate door opens and in walks this lady. Blonde with everything else that counts. She gave me a big smile, and I stopped eating.

"How are you?" she murmured.

"I'm fine now," I said…

From the east gate to the main building is a long, long walk. She smiled her beautiful smile and then slowly moved away—very slowly—I watched the way she moved until she was out of sight. What a walk. I was transfixed. I also wasn't hungry anymore…

Moreover, I forgot to ask her for her pass!

I would later learn that her name was Norma Jean Mortenson. But she will forever be known to all as…Marilyn Monroe.

Dr. Howard Lang

I wanted to get my teeth fixed. I got the name of a good orthodontist, Dr. Howard Lang, and went over to his office and asked him if he could get my teeth straightened. He said it would cost $250. At the time I was working at the Bruin Theatre in Westwood and making $7.00 a week, but I could pay him $5.00 a week. Dr. Lang agreed and explained it would take a couple of years.

When he worked on me, there were times when he would take a pair of pliers to tighten the upper teeth back. It was really painful. Dr. Lang would ask "Are you all right?" to which I would respond, "make it tighter," because I knew my buck teeth were going back into place.

The second year, I ran for Commissioner of Public Relations. I chose as his subject, the President of the United States:

"I am Franklin Delano Roosevelt, President of the United States. I hate war. Eleanor hates war. Cissy and Buzzy hate war. Richard Anderson hates war…"

Won again.

In my senior year it had come time to run for Student Body President. Time to face the same "outlaws" who I lost to at Emerson Junior High School—my opponents. This time, no speech imitations: just a simple talk, stating my qualifications, and asking the student body to vote for me.

They did.

I won.

Dr. Lang had heard from another patient that I was going to make a speech on opening day, as student president. He asked me to come in, looked at my teeth and said, "Tell you what, I'm going to take your braces off."

This is hard to explain: after he did, I felt like I had lost 20 pounds! It was one of those great moments when I felt around with my tongue on the uppers and the lowers. And then of course, Dr. Lang hands me a mirror. I took the mirror and smiled. Because of that, I haven't stopped smiling since!

So I went on stage that day and welcomed everybody back from the summer holidays and I gave them a great big smile, with no small thanks to Dr. Howard Lang. By the way, he used my case as an unusual example for various research laboratories.

Now that Howard Lang had taken care of my teeth it had all changed. I had been aware of some lovely ladies in school, but had also happened to see a movie about high school where the girl kissed the boy (while both were wearing braces) and they both got stuck on the teeth—I didn't want that to happen to me!

In my first year of high school and at the same time beginning to wear my braces, I was having trouble in his Biology class. The teacher, Mr. Copeland, often called on me to talk about the current subject.

There was no question that I had a whole life going—I'd read voraciously and was coming into my own—but somehow—just couldn't get the words out.

In my senior year, I signed on to try again with Biology. And when Mr. Copeland called on me, he reacted to a different Richard Anderson, who answered questions, asked questions and spoke with authority. At the end of the semester, Mr. Copeland would always review the meaning and importance of Biology. In talking to and about his pupils, he said, "Now take Anderson over there—he is different—a different person—he's come out of it—He's with us now."

It was now time to take a drama class—study, do plays, stagecraft, etc. My teacher was Miss Grace Barnes. She made us take on everything—even Shakespeare. Another student and I did a scene

> **University High School**
>
> In recognition of Service to the Student Body
> and as an Expression of its Appreciation
> Awards this Certificate
>
> To **Dick Anderson**
> For **President- Student Body**
> For the term ending **February 4th** **1944**
>
> _Sponsor_   _Principal_

Photo courtesy of Richard Anderson

in front of the class from *The Taming of the Shrew*. According to stage directions, "The Shrew" (and a very pretty one at that) was to sit on my lap. It was the first time that a lady had ever sat on my lap—I could hardly remember my lines!

LINCOLN IN GETTYSBURG

Miss Barnes scheduled me to play Abraham Lincoln in a train on his way to Gettysburg. The whole school was invited that day. They actually built a train cabin set on the stage with a rear screen behind me. You could watch the train go by and hear the sound of the train going along the tracks. And as Mr. Lincoln, I was still working on what is probably the most famous speech in prose ever written, The Gettysburg Address which, at the end of the play, I recite. I was given the American Legion Award for oratory that year.

Many years later, I was invited to Gettysburg and stayed at the town. I had a very interesting time there. I was doing some kind of a commercial for the people at Gettysburg.

But I'll never forget one afternoon when I stood exactly where Lincoln was when he gave the Gettysburg Address (which actually only lasted four minutes).

> "…(T)hat government of the people, by the people, for the people shall not perish from the earth."

It was about slavery.

Afterwards, he said, "I don't think anyone knows what I'm doing here."

It was words. His use of words. His understanding of words. And the way he'd use them.

When he was a boy, his father (who was British) visited the southeast. At night he would often listen to his father talking about things and would think to himself, "I wonder if I could say this and say it differently from the way he said it? It might be interesting."

I once visited the little house where they lived and walked to where he went to high school.

He had understanding; he read a lot of books. By the time he ran for President of the United States, he had developed the reputation for being a very good lawyer. After he had won, with this and all of his hard life experiences, he had been prepared for when the war came.

> "I do the very best I know how, the very best I can; and I mean to keep doing so until the end. If the end brings me out all right, what is said against me won't amount to anything. If the end brings me out wrong, ten angels swearing I was right would make no difference."[1]

ABRAHAM LINCOLN

TENNIS

Playing tennis all through high school: There was a tennis court on the school property. I saved pennies, nickels and quarters, and with my last $8.00, bought a tennis racket at Sontag's drugstore on the corner of Westwood and Lindbrook Drive, which was walking distance from where my family lived.

It's difficult to explain this, but fresh fruit was wrapped around the head of the racket, on the strings. I tell people that today, and they don't know what the heck I'm talking about. Remember there was a depression going on. The companies making the tennis rackets had a reason. They were offering you something to eat if you bought a racket.

After school, with that racket and tennis ball, I'd walk over to a parking lot in Westwood next to a building. I'd hit the ball against the wall of the parking lot to develop my:

A. Strokes;
B. Footwork;
C. Timing.

Hard work.

There was a problem: When a car would come up and wanted to park where I was hitting the ball, all the other spaces were filled, so I would have to step aside. Sometimes,

I would have to wait 20 minutes to a half an hour for someone to leave the parking lot so I could keep hitting.

By doing so I developed a rhythm, a style, and more than anything else, kept my eye on the ball.

Oh, by the way, at the neck of the first tennis racket I ever bought was a picture of Donald Budge. For those who don't know, he was probably the most celebrated player in the history of this game. He brought victories to America at Wimbledon, in the United States, and everywhere he went.

Years later, when I was playing at an exhibition tennis tournament, I was assigned to play doubles with Donald Budge. We got on very well. And by the way, we won that game.

I did get to tell him that his photo was on the first racket I had owned—Budge really liked that.

Several weeks later, I received a call from him to join him in Sydney, Australia, for an exhibition weekend. There was another reason also. It was the first tennis stadium that ever had a roof built on it.

Playing a tournament at UCLA.
Photo courtesy of Richard Anderson

There was one moment on that trip that I'll never forget: We were playing doubles, with Budge playing backhand court. At one point, the ball was served to Budge's backhand (he was known for the best backhand). He hit that ball so hard, so powerfully, and so flat that I could see the handwriting on the ball as it left his racket....

During high school on weekends I would go up to UCLA with hopes that somebody would be there that he could hit balls with. If not, I'd just sit around and watch the UCLA tennis team play there.

One day I happened to be there, just watching the tennis and there was J. D. Morgan, a very well-known tennis player who was the coach of the tennis team and also Bill Ackerman, who at the time was in charge of the whole athletic program at UCLA. One of the players couldn't come so J.D. asked me to "get out there." They invited me often after that.

Mr. Tom Crumpler

Now my brother Bob and I had a ritual on Saturday and Sunday mornings. We would walk up to the courts, play tennis until noon, then we'd go to Westwood Village to have lunch at a shop called Tom Crumpler's, which was across the street from the Westwood Village Theatre.

I'd order a cheeseburger for ten cents and a malt for ten cents. I'd always order the big malt in one of those big, high glasses with creases around them, with whipped cream on top. My brother wanted something a little different. It was a malt that was mixed so much that it was ice cream, rather than a malt. It was smaller, in an iron cup, which was fifteen cents.

I'll never forget Tom Crumpler. He was one interesting character. Always had a cigar in his mouth. Oh, and by the way, it was said that he was from Chicago. We'll leave that alone! He was rough and he was hard, never said much.

While Bob and I were having lunch we would watch those pinball machines near the front door. And adults, all over twenty one, would come in and they used to play the pinball machines because it was a form of gambling, which was against the law: you had to put a nickel into the machine, and you might win something.

I didn't play them. Well, first of all, I never had a nickel. I only had enough money for lunch. But they would put in a nickel and then played the game. Now when some of these guys were playing and they couldn't get the ball where they wanted it to go, they would rap hard on the machine which caused a little sign that came up that says 'tilt,' which meant the game would stop at that point—sure got those old geezers mad! And Tom Crumpler, speaking of mad, would come over and tell them, "If you keep banging on my machine, I'm gonna throw you outta here!"

Years later my brother Bob decided, while we were in Westwood Village, to stop by to see if Tom was still running the place. And there he was...cigar in the mouth. By now, we had had success in our lives, me in movies, Bob a known radio announcer at KABC.

I said "Hello, Tom..."

He looked at us up and down for what felt like an hour then muttered "You wanna buy the place?"

Peter Lawford

One Saturday morning I was waiting to play tennis as no one had shown up yet when someone asked me, "Want to hit some balls?"
"Sure."
I said, "Hello, my name is Dick Anderson."
He says, "I'm Peter Lawford," and tells me, "I'm from England."
"Are you in school out here?"
"No I'm not really doing too much. Actually, I'm an actor."
"Why don't you go down to the Village Theatre? Maybe you could get a job down there as an usher."
He did just that and he got a job at the Fox Village Theater in Westwood Village.

The Bruin Theatre

Then about four or five months later Peter gives me a call one day and says to me: "Dick, I got an acting job with director Henry Hathaway over at 20th Century Fox, so I'm leaving. Get down here and talk to Mr. Clarke and take my job!"
I was busy with other things so my brother Bob went to the place and took the job, Three months later, he called to tell me that there was a job at the Bruin Theater across the street.
Next time I saw Peter Lawford, we were both under contract to Metro-Goldwyn-Mayer.
All Bob and Peter had to do was chop tickets. Two times a week, however, I had to change the marquee. Let me explain: It would be after the last show started at night, climbing a ten-foot ladder, changing the letters and the electric lights behind them. Usually it took about two hours.
My job improved when they asked me to work full time seven days a week chopping tickets at the front door, and no longer having to change the marquee. Whew! When I look back at changing that marquee on a ten-foot ladder on four legs, trying to find a way to reach out and balance it on just two legs, I just shake my head. I could have ended up dead, or in a hospital.
After an eight buck raise I went down on a trolley to Oviatt's in

Los Angeles, the finest suit maker in the world and bought my first suit.

There was a ritual: while chopping tickets, matinee and evening at The Bruin, at some point one of the usherettes would come up to me and say, "Richard, it's happening again," and she'd go up and take my place at the gate until I got back.

I'd slip into the theatre quickly, watching the screen.

And the piano music would start to play that song, and I'd hear the actor say: "I told you never to play that song."...a moment later in would walk Ingrid Bergman.

They'd play the scene, she leaves, and Bogart picks up his drink, takes a sip and says "Of all the gin joints in the world, she had to come into this one."

For those of you who don't know, they took a survey about the most popular movie of all time. Look it up and I think you'll know the answer.

It so happened I started playing on the keys myself. No lessons. Still playing like this.

CHAPTER TWO:
THE M-G-M YEARS (PART ONE)

METRO-GOLDWYN-MAYER

Upon graduating high school, I made an appointment to see Ralph Wadsworth, the President of University High School, to ask if he would kindly write me a letter, which I could take to the Metro-Goldwyn-Mayer offices in Culver City. I had nine months left before going into the army and wanted to get a job to see how films were made at that "Dream Factory" of the world at the studios in Culver City, because it was closer to home. I also knew it was the best studio in town.

I met a Mr. B___ at the Thalberg Building. He read the letter and he says "Whaddya want to do in the movie business?."

I replied, "Well, I'd like to be an actor, later maybe a producer"

He smirked. (The man didn't know who he was talking to, I thought!). I took a deep breath and kept silent.

Mr. B___ said, "Okay, we'll put you in the messenger department."

Four weeks later, after running messages all over the lot, I was invited by a Mr. Ziegler, who was the manager of the publicity department, to work there. Located on the fourth floor of the Washington Boulevard building with the columns on it, in what was called the clipping room.

That building is still there on Washington Boulevard. I drive by it on the way to the airport often, with memories of earlier days. The job included clipping newspaper and magazine articles from publications all around the world: subject MGM, and then taking them downstairs to Howard Strickling's office, Director of Publicity for the studio. When not doing that, I was the one who was told from downstairs to take the visitors around the lot.

AT TIMES: "WHERE'S ANDERSON?"

I would slip away from the clipping room for maybe 20 or 30 minutes at a time to go down to the sound stages and find out how movies were made...and how the stars did their works.

And to just get a glimpse of the stars while they were working.

One day I visited on the soundstage where Lana Turner was working and slipped in hearing this romantic music. It turned out, I learned the studio assigned a young lady from the messenger department to play music for her all day. I used to go back and one day, as she walked toward her dressing room, she smiled at me. She was on the top of the list at the time at MGM, along with Clark Gable, Gene Kelly, etc.

That made a lot of sense to me because I thought when you're acting before a camera, you'd have music behind you. So when I stood in front of a camera for the first time years later, I was all upset when I started talking: "Where's the music?" Later on, I'll tell you a story about the first time I stood in front of a camera.

On those journeys I would "visit" Jane Powell, Vera Ellen, Ava Gardner, Elizabeth Taylor, Jean Simmons. But one of them got away (retired): Greta Garbo.

As I was walking back one time I saw Robert Taylor. I approached him and told him I thought he did a great job in *Camille* (1936), to which he seemed pleasantly surprised.

"I'll have to see that one again," he told me.

One day I went down to a different place, the rehearsal stage where Gene Kelly and Fred Astaire were doing a dance together for *Ziegfeld Follies* (1945).

I was sitting in a corner. The only time they did one together. They shot it six times already. No luck.

Kelly looks up and says, "I'll get you this time."

He was talking to one of the light technicians:

"I'll get it right this time."

From the voice up above:

"Are you on?"
They did the dance. The director said "Print!"
Kelly held up his hand...silver dollar was dropped on it.

Louis B. Mayer

MGM was run by a man named Louis B. Mayer. He had many sides to him. It was all a family—Metro was a family. Mr. Mayer liked the idea of family life. They'd have baseball games and the studio employees would go there. He considered MGM to be a family venture. His mother was one of the people he admired most. If you got sick, or caught a cold, there was the chicken soup from Louie's mother's recipe, bubbling on the stove in the kitchen! And so these kind of things happened on the lot.

He couldn't make a picture if he tried. But Mr. Mayer had some amazing qualities and talents. He had an instinct for talented people. The actors were put under contract if they had a certain individual look and personality. And the top guy was Robert Taylor. In the 40 years or so he was there, he did everything.

That's the way they made the pictures.

Now on one occasion after I had just started working at M-G-M under acting contract, while I was standing by the front gate waiting for a friend, out comes Mr. Mayer from the Thalberg Building with a gang of four men behind him. They all turn the corner:

Ken Hollywood (fittingly named), the security officer at the front gate there, looked at me and said, "Wow, Richard, here comes the boss." He was heading straight for the commissary (or barber shop). He looks at me, STOPS, and stares:

Seems like an hour. Just stares. The men behind...rolling their eyes, set their eyes up in the sky: "Here we go again...

I said, "Mr. Mayer, is there somethi...

"No, no, no, no. I like your face." Off he went to get a shave in the barber shop.

At MGM, everything was categorized. An actor's qualifications were to look a certain way, be a certain age, have a certain demeanor or else they would say, "This is not a Metro actor" and would thereby have no interest. Luckily, I passed the audition!

Camp Roberts

At the end of 1944 I was called into the army and was assigned to Camp Roberts for basic training. After I had completed about six weeks of infantry training, a medical problem was discovered and they put me on hold until they could find a new assignment.

To keep busy, I applied for a job selling tickets at the movie theatre on the base. Sitting next to me in the box office was a man who became a friend whose name was Francis Murphy, and who was running the camp newspaper, The Camp Roberts Dispatch.

While chopping tickets one day, Murph told me in civilian life he was a newspaperman for the Portland Oregonian up north and I told him about my work at MGM. When he heard that, he asked if I would like to work at the camp newspaper and so was transferred there and became their sportswriter.

As Camp Roberts Sportswriter.
Photo courtesy of Richard Anderson.

William Randolph Hearst

One day at Camp Roberts we got into a station wagon with Miss Izzie, who was a civilian and who was assigned to camp. She took them around when they had to do things. She wanted to do something on the subject of the places where the soldiers could go on the weekends. With time off, they could go to San Miguel, which had a hotel which holds a lot of early history about American Indians and so forth.

Glenn Harmon in the office said, "Well, what about William Randolph Hearst...the castle he owns out there in San Simeon?"

Prior to this incident, Norman, the photographer in the office who used to take me with him, had taken some pictures with his four-by-five camera. They couldn't believe it that he was able to get the General's plane, an L5, as well as his pilot. He flew over San Simeon, which was very close to Camp Roberts.

He came back with 3 or 4 wonderful pictures of the three sides, the three buildings. So someone said, "Let's send them to the old man." So Murph sent them to the castle and sure enough, we received a letter three days later signed by William Randolph Hearst.

In the letter he said, "These pictures are the best pictures of the "Rancho" (which he called it) that were ever taken. Thank you for them. As for printing them in your paper, that would be okay, but don't go into details," and in the closing sentence, "Please come and visit me."

So Izzie, Elaine Harmon, who was the WAC (short for the Woman's Army Corps) who worked in our office, Murph, Norman and myself got in the car and drove over to San Simeon, which was probably an hour's drive from Camp Roberts. We arrived at the turn where you go into the front entrance of San Simeon and there were all these beautiful flowers and animals of all kinds running around. And there, from a distance, was a rather tall, elderly man with his hat on, with a woman, just the two of them waiting. So we arrived, stopped, got out of the car and approached him:

(With a high, thin voice): "How do you do? How do you do? Welcome. I enjoyed your pictures very much."

He shook my hand and everyone's hand. I was a Tech Corporal, so he looked at me on both sides.

"Very nice, very nice. Now Dorothy (who appears to be running the house) is coming down the steps and she is going to show you around the Rancho. Meanwhile, thank you very much."

The lady standing with him was smiling and laughing and looking us all over. I recognized her as Marion Davies, a famous screen star and who was Mr. Hearst's companion.

Dorothy showed us everything, opened the doors everywhere, including the big, big swimming pool. And facing the ocean were two cannons which Murph said were from the Spanish-American War in 1898. He had those two cannons brought over and put there to remind him just how much he had to do with us going to war to free the country, Cuba. It was pretty well known that his newspapers had plenty to say on the subject.

(I would like to say that TODAY, I am a member with a very distinguished group of citizens on the board of VETERANS PARK CONSERVANCY. I've been a member for twenty years with the purpose of upgrading the facilities on the corner of Wilshire and San Vicente so that the soldiers coming home from the battlefield have a better chance of recovery.

I often think of my platoon. After six weeks they were shipped to be assigned to the Battle of the Bulge, being outnumbered, and with bad weather, too overcast for planes to help with the many casualties. I wanted in a small way to give something back for possibly half of my platoon who were likely killed).

I was discharged fifteen months later, as a sergeant, and returned to work to MGM in the spring of '46.

WALTER HUSTON

With my military experience, I began writing articles for publications, and still taking important visitors around the sets and occasionally having lunch with them in the commissary. On one occasion I was excited to learn that I was chosen to give Walter Huston, one of America's most famous actors, a tour. I made a special point to show him the whole MGM lot:

Started on Lot One: stages, special effects lab, the film laboratory.

Lot 2: All the outdoor sets.

Lot 3, Andy Hardy

Lot 4, Tarzan's African jungles,

Lot 5, L. B. Mayer's horses, Fred Astaire's horses, studio horses.

At the end of my tour Huston said:

"Well thank you, young man."

"It was an honor, sir. Mr. Huston. I consider you the finest actor of the first 50 years of the twentieth century, and I'd like to ask you a question."

"Well, well, what is your question?"

"Well, I'm trying to be an…"

"Nothing to it, my boy. Put on a good show and always travel first class.'"

What he said stayed with me.

JOHN HUSTON

Years later, we were in a warehouse shooting the first *Six Million Dollar Man* two-hour movie which I was producing. I had heard that John Huston, Walter Huston's son, was shooting in a warehouse next door, so I turned to the assistant director and I said "I'm going to be gone twenty minutes. Tell the cameraman to move a little slower with the lights." I invited an actor that was working with us, Marty Landau, to come…he still talks about it every time I see him.

Huston was in a wheelchair and had an oxygen mask on. I was introduced to him and in the conversation, mentioned I had once met his father.

Huston's head dropped in reaction.

I waited, then said, "When I asked your father some advice on becoming an actor, he said 'Nothing to it, my boy. Put on a good show, and always travel first class.'"

John, without missing a beat SHOT BACK:

"And I see that you have."

Angelica Huston

Talk about irony and genetics…Years later while attending Robert Altman's memorial at the Director's Guild, I noticed that Angelica Huston, the daughter of John Huston was present, excused myself and walked over to introduce myself.

There was a big, strong guy standing there and as I approached, he stopped me. It was her husband, Robert Graham, a famous sculptor. I told him to calm down and told him that I wanted to ask his wife a question. He backed off (not much), and as I approached her, she said:

"Hello, Richard."

I have met many people but when I saw her eyes, so romantic, so sparkling, so full of kindness, I could hardly talk. I eventually said:

"There's something I want to tell you. I once met your grandfather."

She said "Oh?" and dropped her head.

I told her what my question was to him when I asked about acting, to which he responded "Put on a good show, and always travel first class."

She looked up at me, without skipping a beat, she said:

"And I see that you have."

I took a deep breath. Ah…family.

More About Louis B. Mayer

Having lunch one day with a guest who had been involved with the invention of radio. Had paid the bill and was about to leave and show them the lot when from his private dining room in the commissary came L. B. Mayer. He was always told when there was an important person was visiting the studio…

Stopped at the table…long pause…then:

"The people decide. They are the ones that have the clear minds to decide the big issues in this country."

With that he walked away.

Now another time, while under contact for the studio, I was on the set while acting in a picture called *Scaramouche* (1952).

When Mr. Mayer came visiting and heard director George Sidney say to him, "I want to get this crane for a long shot and need your ok to rent it."

Mayer shouted "BUY IT! But if anyone asks if I okayed it, I'll deny it!"

It's been said that Louis B. Mayer was the best actor on the lot.

LIFE AT METRO

People would ask him for a raise, and he'd get down on his knees and cry.

"You don't seem to understand the pressures I'm under" and so forth.

"My boy, you're my son. I've never had a son."

He said that to Robert Taylor when he asked him for a raise. His agent couldn't get anywhere with him, so Taylor, considering that he was working with all the big directors, decided to give it a try.

Mayer sat down, ten minutes, talking, crying, everything.

Taylor left, called his agent and the agent asks what happened.

He says "I didn't get the raise, but now I've got a father…"

Also said the boss could not make a movie BUT had an inborn instinct for talent. Had them all around him. How about Irving Thalberg?

Lana Turner was highly underrated. People don't really understand that in those days, how hard the work was. The lighting—the time it takes. The lighting on your eyes could cause a lot of problems.

And there were those big Technicolor cameras. You see that thing coming at you and it's like a freight train. And the days were long. Gable was the only one on the lot who said in his contract, "I go home at five." People said there were a lot of social things going on.

Yeah, but I'll tell you the actors were mostly working. Long hours.

Myrna Loy retired in the east in her latter days. Roddy McDowall had been at the studio as well. He was interviewing people, taking pictures and doing that on the side in later life. "Little Roddy." Remember him?: *HOW GREEN WAS MY VALLEY* (1941). He visited her and he asks, "Myrna, got a question for you. You were the highest grossing actress at the studio for three straight years. But what was it really like?"

She hesitated for a minute, and then she said "IT WAS LIKE A SWEAT FACTORY."

That's the way they made the pictures, and they wanted everybody to look great. Then Billy Wilder does *Sunset Boulevard* (1950) at Paramount, about the May–December romance between Bill Holden and Gloria Swanson. Louie comes up and asks him "How dare you make a picture like that? How dare you do such a thing? Our actors are all, you know, they're…"

He was at the end. He was living in a world that no longer was.

But as it turns out, look at how his movies are faring now. We're into "yesterday" today, I'm telling you. Audiences want these stories, they want to hear about what went on and of course everybody's watching Turner Classic Movies, even kids…

Bought Sight Unseen

Barney Balaban, who in later years was president of Paramount Studios, once told this story about his mother:

She came home one day in Brooklyn with her kids and she says, "I've just seen something that I've never seen before in my life."

"What is it, Ma?"

"I went up to this place, it says something about an Office…"

Someone says "The box office?"

She says "Yes, the box office. And I put down my 15 cents, and it's the first time I put any money down without knowing what I saw."

And that's what movies are: something you buy without actually seeing them first. This is what Mayer and all of the studio heads and creative people have always had to deal with, which will likely never change. Easy to second guess, not so easy to carry out successfully.

The Actors Laboratory

After being discharged from the army, veterans had the right to return to their former job after they were discharged. However, upon my return from the army I quit my job at the Metro studio as I had the opportunity, after having auditioned and been accepted, to join the Actor's Laboratory in Los Angeles.

The Actor's Lab was an offshoot of The Group Theater. It later became the Actor's Studio, headed by Lee Strasberg. I studied there for a year under the G.I. Bill of Rights. It was all based on Konstantin Stanislavsky's theories about "The Method."

To stay on an even keel, I make it a point to think about what Walter Huston had told me, which was most of the time…the theories.

Marilyn Monroe and John Garfield would come around and watch some of the acting.

I remember when I went in to audition for it, Rose Hobart, an actress who had appeared with Fredric March in *Dr. Jekyll and Mr. Hyde* (1932) was there in the front and she asks "Why do you want to be an actor?" I was stuck for an answer. She was trying to warn me!

Sam Levene, who had originated the role of Nathan Detroit in *Guys and Dolls* on Broadway, directed my audition scene.

They asked me on one audition to come in with a scene with some music behind it, and that's just what I did. At the house I was playing a record to prepare when my mother and father walked in and I stopped.

They said, "What are you doing?"

"Well, I have to do this…"

They said, "What kind of music is that?"

I said, "That's Frank Sinatra."

My Acting Debut

I was in a play while I was at The Actor's Lab, which we did at the Las Palmas Theatre, in which I held a spear. I was a soldier, and was wearing one of the Imperial police helmets.

In the rehearsals I was having a problem with the helmet, as it was the only one I could find at Western Costume, which they said would fit.

It finally got to the point of the one line I had in the play on the night it opened:

"Your Majesty, the lady is arriving..."

With that, the hat fell off!

The opening of my career as a professional actor!

The Long Voyage Home (Play)

While at The Actor's Lab, I also did plays in addition to attending classes. One of them was a wonderful one-act play written by Eugene O'Neill called *The Long Voyage Home*, in which I played a Swedish sailor (with accent).

In the story, the sailor comes back after being at sea, but this year, he's going to buy a farm. Every year before that, he never got that far. All his money went to the bar and the ladies around.

He loved coming to the bar after the sea voyage and again, like they say, nothing really changes...But he's telling them all, "No, I'm not going to do it, THIS TIME I'm going to buy that farm."

Alas, he spends and loses his money yet again. He ends up the same way and he has to go back "...to the old sea again, that I hoped I would never see again."

Eugene O'Neill was that kind of a writer. His stuff was very dark, but I enjoyed it because it gave me the opportunity to play a very fine character. It was the most enjoyable experience I had at The Actor's Lab.

To give you some idea of what I'm attempting to say, I remember a classmate from the Actor's Lab I met on a job years later.

I asked, "How did it go with you after all these years. Did you find The Lab useful?"

"Useful? I arrived at work there to do one scene, when at last the assistant director knocks on my trailer door and says, 'We're ready. Do this fast. We're losing the light.'

"I was on a location...had to climb a hill...started to shoot, couldn't remember a line!"

Didn't work for him either.

Gary Cooper and Ernest Hemingway

High Noon (1952) with Grace Kelly was a beautiful one for Gary Cooper. It brought out a side of him that we hadn't seen before in all of the Westerns he had previously done.

In *For Whom the Bell Tolls* (1943), which took place during the Spanish Civil War, he had a scene with Ingrid Bergman at the end when he had to leave her.

"I have to go, you know how it is."

It just puts you away.

Many writers in the 1930's went over to Paris to work with an American lady named Gertrude Stein who was quite elderly, rich, and was very good with the books that she wrote. A lot of young people came in to learn how to write books. There was a fellow there from the same sort of background as Cooper. His father was a doctor, but he pulled out and went to Paris, France.

Cooper and Hemingway met in Idaho in 1940 and became great friends. They used to go to the middle west, skiing and duck and pheasant hunting and so on.

Hemingway hated the guys in Hollywood. He said "They don't know how to make pictures. They haven't done my pictures right." But when it came to this guy it all changed and they were friends to the end. Hemingway was a great admirer of his because he had the same thing, wanting to do the right works and being strong enough to simply do it.

It turned out, at the end of that story, they were both not well. In those days, all the great actors and actresses like Gable and all of them smoked and drank and, by the time they were 60, they were gone. So this is what was really going on here.

They were on the phone one time towards the end. By this time Hemingway had lost his works, drinking heavily and he was just waiting for the time to shoot himself. His wife tried to get him not to.

Then Ernest had learned that Cooper wasn't well at all either. He called him up and they talked for while about old times. But before hanging up, there was one more thing:

"Papa," says Cooper, as if saying good-bye:

"I bet I beat you to the barn."

Hemingway followed him less than two months later.

Both Cooper and Hemingway inspired me and influenced me in my work in their ability to convey strong emotion, thoughts and ideas through a deceptively simple, minimalist approach in their respective work which I have emulated in my acting performances.

"*The Sun Also Rises is written in spare, tight prose that influenced countless crime and pulp fiction novels and made Hemingway famous.*" [1]

Santa Barbara and Laguna Beach

Upon leaving the Actor's Lab in the spring of 1949, I did a season of summer stock in Santa Barbara and Laguna Beach, later working the street, auditioning at CBS, NBC and ABC radio in Hollywood.

I had heard of an audition for the play *Kind Lady* with Sylvia Sidney at the Lobero Theatre in Santa Barbara. I came in and auditioned and won the featured part, and then they asked me to do another play, a comedy.

Laguna Summer Playhouse Program.
Photo courtesy of Richard Anderson

Richard and supporting actor in the play *Kind Lady*.

Then came a job called *Anna Lucasta* down at Laguna Beach, a leading role. Word came around. It was reviewed by *Variety* and described me as being "Gregory Peck-like."

And it was a wonderful part, that of a Southern boy who falls in love with a woman with a questionable past; I was then asked to do another play there, *Peg O' My Heart*.

Samuel L. Goldwyn

My agent called him and said that Sam Goldwyn wanted to meet me.

Goldwyn was all by himself all the time. He could not work with anybody after attempting to work with Mayer for a short period.

I was glad to meet the man, sitting right in his office, who had made some of the finest movies ever made such as *Best Years of Our Lives* (1946) with Fredric March and Myrna Loy, and *Wuthering Heights* (1939) with Laurence Olivier and Merle Oberon.

I had respect for him. He was of the old school and came across from Warsaw, then part of the Russian Empire, having to walk more than five hundred miles at various points in total. He got off the boat in Nova Scotia, Canada out of fear of being denied entry, then walked another five hundred miles to New York. He would later move to California under better circumstances.[2]

So those fellows were something: gamblers and more than anything, as I said earlier, they respected their movies and took pride in making them.

Lights, Camera, Action! (1950–)

I was still after work, making the rounds on the street, from NBC to CBS to ABC and auditioning for whatever might come up. And then I had heard that a show called *Lights, Camera, Action*, a live show with a large audience, was about to go on the air.

They had auditions at 4:00 pm on Fridays. Then finally one day, I asked myself, "What time is it? It's 2:00 pm. I'll go."

They handed me a comedy script: A boy and a girl meeting in the lobby of a hotel—a blind date—pass each other, sit next to each other, unawares. She drops her purse, he picks it up, and he starts: "Oh, there you are!"

Got applause for it, and judges that were favorable, and they brought me back for the second one. The writers of *Lights, Camera, Action* called me after the first win, to say they had a dramatic skit.

"No way," I said. "Stick with the comedy!"

The approach was very much like today's *Dancing with the Stars*, in an auditorium at NBC filled with an audience who voted the talent on or off. There were four other skits in the competition. After winning the night, I came back two more times and took the grand prize of a weekend trip, all expenses paid, to a posh hotel in La Jolla, AND a role in the next film produced by Edward Small (more about Mr. Small later).

The town was mine: everyone was calling. Billy Wilder was calling about a movie. RKO put me in *Payment on Demand* (1951), with Bette Davis.

They had well-known industry directors and writers as judges. At the end of the third skit for which I won the grand prize, one of the judges came out of the booth, walked over to me, shook my hand, and introduced himself:

"Mr. Anderson, I'm Preston Sturges. I congratulate you on your work," and he gave me a big smile.

For those that are unfamiliar, he was an extraordinary filmmaker who made what are considered to be some of the most wonderful comedies of that time, which can be seen regularly on Turner Classic Movies.

THE VANISHING WESTERNER (1950)

I received a call to play a leading role in *The Vanishing Westerner* (1950) at Republic Studios, which came as a result of my work on Television. A producer over at Republic saw me on it and offered me a job.

"Do you know how to ride a horse?"

"Sure!!" I said. (I hadn't ridden a horse in my life!)

Snowy Baker, the famous Australian sportsman and silent film actor who worked there, got me on a horse and I rode along for four days. I played a romantic part. It was directed by Phil Ford, the nephew of John Ford. I am proud of a plaque that was given to me for the film at my first Western show.

MAMA ROSA (1950):
(FIRST TELEVISION SERIES, CO-STARRING)

I hardly recall it, but it was my first work on film. While shooting, I remember thinking, "Where's the background music?" First lesson in moviemaking: what is seen on-screen is not necessarily what the actor gets while shooting it. Was quite an eye-opening experience for me at the time.

CHAPTER THREE:
THE M-G-M YEARS (PART TWO)

WHO IS "MR. GRANT"?

The writer/producers of *LCA* called me ONE day to tell me that a Mr. Grant had called and wanted to speak to me.

Who was this "Mr. Grant"?

I checked Grant, Grant, in the listings. I found out there was a casting director at Republic named Grant! I called him up with anticipation.

He says "No! I didn't call you. Never heard of you."

Next day the *LCA* Producer called.

"That 'Grant' was CARY Grant."

"Oh...How am I going to get hold of him?"

I got right on it and found out that he was filming a picture at MGM called *Crisis* (1950).

I called the studio, asked for publicity, where a sweet lady named Gloria worked at the office switchboard. I knew her from the time when I was working at the publicity department, after I returned to MGM from the army.

"Gloria, it's Richard Anderson. Could you connect me to the stage where Cary Grant is shooting?"

"All right Dick, but don't tell anybody."

She dials and the phone rings:

"Cary Grant please."

They asked me, "Who's calling?"

I mention that Mr. Grant wants to talk to me and they put him through to me:

"Hallo?"

"Mr. Grant, I'm Richard Anderson. I understand that you called?"

"I certainly did. Richard, my wife Betsy saw you on that screen test show on television and called me in to say 'Look at this man. He is terrific...' and so you were. We both think you are just wonderful! Come out to lunch at the studio. We would like to help you. I'm going to talk with Dore Schary here at MGM about you."

Shortly after, I also met the gifted Betsy Drake (Mrs. Grant).

First Screen Test!

The next week, the phone rang and it was arranged for me to meet with Mr. Schary, the head of the studio, at his office. He mentions that he had heard about me and tells me, "When you're finished shooting (the Bette Davis film for RKO) come out and make a screen test for our producers to look at." After I had finished working, I found a good test scene at Lillian Burns' office at MGM from a movie called *The Cowboy and the Lady* (1938) starring (you guessed it) Gary Cooper:

Scene: A cowboy knocks on the door, a beautiful lady (played by Sally Forrest) opens it, invites him in, excuses herself "to get into something more comfortable" and suggests he makes some drinks. He wanders over to a lady's perfume table, picks up a powder puff, sort of dusts it on his nose, shakes his head and drops it. He goes to the bar, reaches for the ice, tosses several big pieces in the air, catches them in each glass. She comes out of the bedroom with not much on but still quite a bit in these days.

"Let's sit down on the couch here" she says after taking the cocktail.

He starts for the door, stops and says:

"Pardon me Ma'am...but I gotta go."

And does...

The screen test was sent to all the producers. Every one voted for me. I signed a seven-year contract.

So that was quite an experience.

Cary and Betsy (Drake) Grant.
Photo courtesy of Richard Anderson.

AT HOME WITH CARY AND BETSY

That was not the last of Cary and Betsy Grant, however.

Around that period of time, after *Lights, Camera, Action* they would invite me to their home. Only small parties for dinner, no big ones, no more than six. Jean Simmons, Stewart Granger, Irene Selznick, Spencer Tracy, Katherine Hepburn, etc. Quiet evenings. Cary showing movies.

But before my MGM contract, there was a radio program called *New Talent*. They would invite stars to come on to introduce new talent. And this is exactly what happened with me. I was on a show with Cary Grant who introduced me:

"I want to tell you about a wonderful new actor you'll be hearing about…Richard Anderson…"

After the introduction, I did a brief scene.

Through that I received accolades from people in the film business that I hadn't heard from forever, which provided a gratifying sendoff to this most important phase of my career.

Richard Anderson, MGM Contract Player.
Photo courtesy of Richard Anderson.

To quote the studio's most famous publicity line, at MGM I would soon have the opportunity to work alongside what appeared to be "more stars than there are in Heaven."

My Acting "Strategy"

In its heyday, actors just starting out were given supporting roles with leading actors, then second parts, leading up to a shot at a starring role.

Although the system itself began to fall apart, with the resulting overall business decline, my strategy served me well in spite of all. In my desire to gain experience I played *everything* assigned to me.

To continue to work, to stay onscreen required that you took whatever was available. Some actors want to do a certain thing which, one way or another, whether you have your chance at it or it just fades out, you're back to where you started, at best.

At that time, the *life expectancy* of an actor was about seven years on average. It probably hasn't changed much today.

Although I had looked forward to playing lead roles at MGM, I was seen by the studio as a "good, dependable supporting player," so my option continued to be picked up as a result. They knew they could rely on me.

Unbeknownst to me at the time, I was being provided with training for my later work on television, where it's all about getting it done quickly.

Marilyn Monroe

I was on a loan out to 20th Century Fox for a film called *A Life of Her Own* (1950). I bumped into Cary Grant on the lot where he was shooting *Monkey Business*. "Hey Richard, meet me at the commissary for lunch at noon."

I walked into the commissary and there was Cary sitting with director Howard Hawks and a beautiful blonde lady whom, it appeared was also in the picture…

In fact, I recognized her from that day years before at the east gate of University High, while fulfilling my duties as commissioner of Public Safety. Back then her name was Norma Jean. Cary stood up, shook my hand and said:

"Richard, I'd like you to meet Marilyn Monroe."

She smiled and said, to my surprise:

"I saw you on Santa Monica Blvd and Wilshire driving your car. It was a convertible blue car" (The top must have been down—always liked the sun). "You were serious. You looked so serious."

"Well, frankly, I'm always serious when driving a car...a dangerous machine," I said.

Later on in the lunch, when people came over to the table to chat with Cary and Howard, I had my chance. I said very quietly:

"Marilyn, You know, we've met before."

She looked at me, suddenly serious and said:

(A cold) "No."

On a later occasion, *Photoplay Magazine* put on an awards dinner at Ciro's, at which Marilyn had won and was featured on the cover for "Bright Young Women That Are Going Places." I was invited, having been listed as one of the "Bright Young Men That Are Going Places." Everybody individually stood up after dinner was over, whereupon she saw me.

She came to the edge of the stage, looked down at me where he was sitting and with that matchless smile and slight move of her body said:

"Yes, Richard, I remember you!"

Vulnerable, dazzling. Dead at thirty six.

ACROSS THE WIDE MISSOURI (1951)

Clark Gable, folks. My third movie of the twenty four I did at MGM.

Gable had great discipline. The movie was successful when it came out, but Gable was sort of going this way a bit. After the war, he didn't really hit the same way, but he was still Gable.

William Wellman directed it on location in Colorado.

I watched Gable the first morning with his leading lady, Maria Elena Marques. He wanted to rehearse, knowing that what it took for him to look easy and confident on screen was to work hard on the DIALOGUE. They rehearsed for an hour.

Actress Meryl Streep said it when she won a Golden Globe Award. She said, "My mother told me when I was scared all the time to come in and also 'Do the work.' I'm home alone, and I'm home alone a lot. You know what I'm doing? I'm learning those lines, so

I don't have to think of them in front of a camera. That's lonely work."

Gable knew that. I knew it too but thought it would become easier as you gain fame and fortune. But there was the KING OF FILM rehearsing and not just figuring he could just come out and wing it.

I had an opportunity to talk to him a little bit about films and stuff and he gave me some good advice, like, "If you want something, why, you're gonna have to give something when you go upstairs to talk to them."

I had a scene with him. We were both on horseback and we're riding over to this fort. Now, the camera is far back, it's just a long shot and they said:

"All right. Roll 'em. Action!"

He says, "Well, I want to tell you that…abpt…abit…"

And I filled in. I said, "You want me to go over to the fort?" I said to myself, "My God, Clark Gable blows lines?"

Esther Williams was coming up and they decided they were going to do some of the swimming movies. And they called Gable in to make the test with her. He came and it was a short scene. He's looking at his watch and then finally he does what he does so well. He takes her arm, he sweeps her back, turns her low, gives her a big kiss and then he says, "I got plenty I gotta do today."

Gable had in his contract that 5:00 pm good bye was all. But he did come in to help out. It got Esther Williams a contract and a long career in films. They didn't hesitate to use the studio sets. In this case it was important that they sell it to the money people in New York, to help sell her as a swimming star. So Gable said "I'll help you," and he followed up on it.

As you may remember, Gable did a lot of pictures with Spencer Tracy. They tried to find combinations: Tracy and Hepburn. And certainly they did it with William Powell and Myrna Loy. They wanted to give something like a series on the screen. They kept coming back: Andy Hardy with Mickey Rooney. It worked. People couldn't wait to see the next one. Gable did pictures where they put Tracy against him.

There was *Boom Town* (1940), an oil well picture. Claudette Colbert and Hedy Lamarr were in it too. And Tracy was quoted as saying of Gable, "There's nothing like him. Nothing like him. He's the best."

I'll tell you about another incident in *Missouri*. We all used to meet at night. I have a picture of Gable, William Wellman and myself sitting at a long table eating dinner. That's how it was. We lived in a tent. Gable had his own little place, as did Jimmy Whitmore and I think Ricardo Montalban had one too. But I was just starting, it was my first job there, so I'm living in a tent.

There was a big scene on a big hill and these guys that were coming down the hill. It was another sequence but it was just a lot of the men coming down. And I was standing there watching it and this older guy who had been talking about everything, what goes on in Westerns and stuff, I saw him fall off his horse. He fell off and he stood up, got right back on the horse and kept riding down. Now, that night at the poker game I asked where he was—and they said that he broke his back. He finished the ride till he got downhill. That's how these guys were.

SCARAMOUCHE (1952)

We were shooting *Scaramouche* in San Francisco. It was the first shot of the movie, which George Sidney was directing. George was fun, he had a sense of humor. We shot in the park there which was used for the forest scenes. I'm on a horse waiting and up rides Stewart Granger.

He asks me, "Where's my lady?" (Eleanor Parker)

And I say:

"I mislaid her."

They showed the preview. The audience roared!

Later on, when we were preparing to shoot the fencing scene with Mel Ferrer, I was in my costume and so forth and was getting ready to go on.

Just before I'm ready to go on, this lady comes over and looks at me. I had met her before in makeup. She came with an electric razor and she starts shaving my chest.

I said, "What the ____ are you doing? Are you nuts?"

She said, "No, no, actors are not allowed to show hair on their chest." She was very serious.

Movies have changed.

SPENCER TRACY

Spencer Tracy was difficult, according to L.B. Mayer: "Difficult man."

I did a picture with him. In the first scene I had with him in *The People Against O'Hara* (1951), I was just waiting and he walks in. He had on a short white coat, like he was a medic.

And he just quietly walks in, slowly. He looks at me, "Yeah, well (mumbles to himself)." He barely spoke. What he was doing was sizing the scene up, sizing ME up and everybody else.

He evidently did that all the time when he came in to rehearse. He mumbled the lines and then left. Then we'd shoot—and it was one take.

Two things about Spencer Tracy:

I was in the barbershop one day and he came in. He had a barber who did his hair. He would say, "Look, don't cut the sideburns. Don't cut 'em at all. Women like that."

I'd come down on the set to watch him. The scene was in his office behind his desk talking on the phone. I remember he was saying to the director, John Sturges:

Spencer Tracy, Richard and Diana Lynn in *The People Against O'Hara* (1951).
Photo courtesy of Richard Anderson.

"Wait a minute, these words...uh, uh, let's do it this way."

He did: he refocused the whole scene and he made it better. And then he says:

"All right."

So they say "Quiet! Action!"

First take. Tracy picks up the phone:

"Well, I don't know, Bill, if we should do that. If he...Oh, nuts, I blew the line."

Silence for a minute. Sturges says "CUT!"

Tracy says: "Uh oh, somebody's gonna call the production office, call Louie B. Mayer and tell him Tracy's forgetting his lines again."

This is what they do sometimes, you see. The production office calls down to the stages at 11:00 am to see if they got the first shot.

Dream Wife (1953)

Cary Grant had asked me to appear in *Dream Wife* with him and Deborah Kerr "for good luck"...a comedy about marriage.

My scene: Three men sitting in an office. All talking about marriage and how difficult it could be.

"Not so" say I. "I have a solid, peaceful, happy, fulfilled time. We dine out, we go to movies and sometimes the three of us travel together."

"THE THREE OF YOU?!" Cary asks.

"Yes. My mother-in-law lives with us."

Escape from Fort Bravo (1953)

One day early on I was walking around the commissary when I saw William Holden.

I looked at him and he started mumbling, and I thought "Wait a minute, what's going on?"

Then I got it:

Holden had read the script and was playing a scene he does with me. That's how preparation goes with these stars, they make it so personal.

I learned more about Westerns from him than I ever learned from anybody before or since, which I later used—and believe me, I've done a lot of Westerns.

I learned so much from Bill there. I'd never seen anyone do things in front of the camera as he did in *Escape From Fort Bravo*. He did not use a stuntman for anything we did in the ten weeks we worked on *Fort Bravo*, where many others did, and I stupidly tried to do the same.

He wanted a horse that was a THOROUGHBRED, he didn't want a studio horse. Studio horses knew what they wanted to do. He wanted to deal with this horse, and DID. He insisted on getting one and they gave him one.

In one of the scenes where the army is surrounded by Indians, one of them shoots me with an arrow successfully.

Now, there's a way they do that which is kind of interesting. They had put a piece of wood against my chest, then they put a nail there, where they attach an open piece of wire and send the wire up to a crew member sitting high on top of a ladder with a bow and arrow and the arrow is attached to the wire. Then he blows the arrow and it comes down and he hits me on the chest, while mounted on the horse.

They were doing that and he got it all set up and rigged to say a few lines and then the arrow comes down. They wanted to rehearse it and I said "Don't rehearse it. Let's just shoot it." But they insisted on rehearsing it and...

When they shot it, that horse went straight up in the air... STRAIGHT UP in the air. I didn't have time for my legs to hold in, I just SLID down and I fell off the horse. The horse went up on two legs and I was told he had missed my face by two inches with one of his hoofs.

Well, that's an interesting story because I've had two or three incidents like that in my life where I was so grateful to be alive and when things got really tough, I'd lean back and think about when I was lying there with a hoof not three inches away from my face.

I quickly got up and they said "Are you okay?"

I responded, "Get the horse," and I got right back on, which is what they say you always HAVE to do.

A couple of sequences later where the soldiers have to go down a steep hill, stuntmen would first walk down and move all the rocks. It was a steep ride and a horse might hit one.

They always did that, except Bill and I were ahead of the group, going full gallop. The cameras were behind us. Going down I promised myself, "I'll let a stuntman do this from now on." I felt grateful, fortunate and was going to stick to the dialogue.

A lot of actors want to do it all themselves. You can do that, but you know you have stunt directors. One shouldn't try to be a hero in that kind of thing. And I was fortunate, very fortunate in this case.

Another incident in *Fort Bravo* was when we had to go up a narrow trail along a mountain…

We'd call it a hill, but it was really a mountain. I have a picture of it. I looked to the left and I said, "This is really tough," because it was a very narrow trail. Just before we started, the wrangler came over to me and says:

"Richard, there's something I need to tell you."

"Tell me what?"

And he said, "I'll walk up a little with you, when you get there."

We got up there. It was WAY down.

He then revealed, "Your horse is 75% blind."

I said, "You son-of-a-bitch."

They do that. It was all a plan. It's a joke. Isn't that wonderful, though? And he said it absolutely straight. He says "That horse is 75% blind…"

Okay, now that brings up something that happened to me back when we moved to California.

We lived at 2030 Pelham Avenue, and the house was situated where you walk up a step and to go in the front door in the front of the driveway. There's a little patio adjacent to the front door. The garage goes along the wall and the fellow that owned the house had a little Whippet car and backed out every morning to go to work.

I was sitting with my bottom above the stairs and my legs were sticking out onto the driveway there. And I wasn't paying attention or anything, I was just musing, so to speak, and suddenly I lifted my legs off the driveway onto the step as Fred Lanson's car backed off…If I had left them on three seconds later, I'd have lost my legs.

Never forgot. It's a point of remembrance for being grateful.

Just This Once with Richard and Peter Lawford.
Photo courtesy of Richard Anderson.

JUST THIS ONCE (1952)

Sidney Sheldon was on the MGM lot early in his career, writing original stories, mainly comedies, and this was one of them. It wasn't a big picture. The movie was about two men, myself and Peter Lawford, who were in love with Janet Leigh. It was fun. Don Weis directed it.

What was unusual was that the crew was particularly interested… watching it because it was a fun story. One of the crew came up and asked, "Are you going to get her or not?"

ALFRED HITCHCOCK

I played an extra for him, actually, just a fellow sitting way in the back, first job, no dialogue for a couple of days when just starting out. And there was Hitchcock sitting waaay down at the end. And I just watched him. He was falling asleep during the time.

He planned his film. He was trained to really plan everything and he had it all planned. Hitch's movie making formula: get the best actors and get on with it.

Sometime during my MGM period, I went to his house one time for an event. He lived on the golf course in Bel Air. I got an invitation to come up, as I recall, with some friends of mine that knew him. The understanding was that he was going to preview his movie down at the Hollywood Paramount. If memory serves, it was one of the three that he had done with Grace Kelly. So I went up there and walked in.

Mrs. Hitchcock was there. She greeted me, "How do you do?"

There were some well-known people there including Grace, whom I had actually known a little at Metro, and a few others like that. But a whole lot of people were all going to come.

So he came over and said,

"Good evening, Mr. Ander*shon*, we meet again."

"How do you do, Mr. Hitchcock."

"Would you like a drink?"

"Yeah, fine. I just love your place here."

"Yes, it's very comfortable."

And then the time came, and he had a bus for all of us to take down to the theatre. I'll never forget this, if you want to talk about. We were talking about everything's fixed. And his wife, by the way, was an editor. She did all that back stuff. They were together in England when they made all those pictures before he came to the U.S. So then we were ready to go, and Hitch walks over to me and he says:

"Mr. Ander*shon*, I think it's time we get into the bus to come down to see my picture that we are going to show to *THE IDIOTS!*"

That was his description of the audience. Is that something? He lived in another world. He had a great sense of humor! He always wore a tie and a coat. There are a lot of stories about Hitchcock.

But Hitchcock finally came out in print and said, "My favorite of them all, my favorite actor is Cary Grant." Remember that scene in *North by Northwest* (1959) where he's running through the cornfield with the airplanes behind him?

Hitchcock was a a very organized director. I didn't work with him directly, but years later I was on an episode of *The Alfred Hitchcock*

Hour called "Who Needs An Enemy?" I would see him on the lot when I would go to do some voice over work, pick-ups and things like that. Hitchcock was on the set one day and I came over. He was just doing post-production on his series.

"Mr. Hitchcock, good morning."

"Good morning."

"I just want to tell you how much I admire the show."

"Thank you very much, Mr. Ander*shon*."

"And also for the work."

"Well, thank you for the compliment."

But every day he'd go to work. He had an office there at Universal. I had a dressing room right near him. He had a chauffeur bring him in.

As he'd go in, he'd look at the sound stages, he'd look and he'd say, "Well, back to prison."

THE STORY OF THREE LOVES (1954)

The Story of Three Loves was just that. In the movie, I had a scene where I started playing the piano and singing. In the first rehearsal, Kirk Douglas is looking out the window, about to talk in a scene with Pier Angeli, and heard me singing. In the middle of the rehearsal he stopped and said "Hey Richard, I like the way you sing."

Under my contract with MGM, they had us going to classes, dancing, singing, fencing, and playing various musical instruments. If one of us broke through, it paid for everybody else. Debbie Reynolds was one of them. But when I reminded her of that recently, she replied, "We were all stars."

I like to play the piano. When the film came on again recently, I got a lot of letters on it.

Today it looks like kind of a "movie of the old days." Same way pictures used to be made, kind of European.

A Great Lady Has an Interview (1954)

I was one of four actors who made a short subject along with their biggest star, Lana Turner. MGM decided to make some short subjects and show them on television.

Hermes Pan, who did extensive work with Fred Astaire, directed what we would call a ten-minute musical. It was a remake of a segment from *Ziegfeld Follies* (1945) which starred Judy Garland. The men are singing and then she comes out and we dance with her. Finally at the end we put her up on our shoulders. It hasn't been seen on television. *But* thanks to the folks at TCM, I am proud to own a copy of it now!

Brief Marriage

I was briefly married while in my twenties. We could see that it was an unwise youthful decision and decided to go our separate ways both appropriately and amicably.

Hollywood Park

One time while I was still under contract to MGM, Cary Grant and his wife Betsy Drake invited me with some friends to an event at Hollywood Park where Grant was on the Board. As we were about to go up on the elevator, they stopped:

Someone said, "Wait a minute, there's this man who wants to go up."

He was an older gentleman, wore a suit but with pants too long, the cuffs were over the shoes, and the coat of the suit was too big. Just shuffling along.

They all waited until he got into the elevator.

Silence. They start going up the elevator. Silence.

Suddenly he says:

"FIVE DAY WEEK!"

Silence, then louder.

"Five days a week. No Saturdays. No more Sundays. Gone forever. Five day week."

"Short sleeves to shirt sleeves in three generations."

"The first generation makes it, the second one spends it, and the third one starts all over."

That was it. The elevator stops, opens, and out he goes.

"Who was that, Cary?" I asked.

"That was Harry Warner," he said.

That's all he said. I guess he wanted to talk to somebody and that was it.

Well, it turns out the studio unions had just turned everything into five days instead of six. When I started there it was six days a week and they could work till Saturday night and still have to be there at 5 am Monday. Sometimes they go over into Sunday. So that's what he meant, that they were saying "Five day week."

He was the one most respected by the bankers. Jack Warner, that was a different story. Jack was a "picture maker." Harry was the real essence of them in terms of finances.

These men were all tough guys, particularly the ones that ran the studios. It was really all about numbers, first. But also, they took pride in their movies. They were willing to spend money if they saw something going well. They'll put more money into it, and risk that, because the risk is you hope the audience will go see their films. So that was the thing about them.

You have to understand the one thing they had was something that everybody talks about now: pride of ownership. Six guys who had their own personal vision and set the pattern for some time afterwards: Darryl Zanuck, Harry Cohn, Sam Warner, Louie Mayer, Adolph Zukor and Carl Laemmle. And I'll give you an example: In my last year at the Metro studio, I was hauled in to do a picture called *Forbidden Planet*.

Forbidden Planet (1956)

Of the 24 pictures I did at MGM, the one that surprised everyone was *Forbidden Planet*. It was made on one stage, shot in twenty days. I honestly thought it was just another job. That was my twenty-fourth picture for them.

My first day on the set, there's Walter Pidgeon, who I thought

As Chief Quinn in *Forbidden Planet*.
Photo courtesy of Richard Anderson.

was one of the best actors of them all, Anne Francis, and all the rest. And then—"What the hell's going on here?"—in comes this robot.

(Robby the robot was initially played by actor Frankie Darro, who had appeared in many films during the 1930s and 1940s as a young leading man. Due to some type of conflict he was later replaced in post-production by actor Marvin Miller, who provided the memorable voice of Robby).

The script was based on Shakespeare's play *The Tempest* from a story by Irving Block, who did visual effects for numerous Sci-Fi films of the period, and Allen Adler. Nicholas Nayfak was the producer in the "B" unit of MGM, which produced the second-billed features which played after the "A" productions, and had been trying to get this made for a long time. The 'A' unit gets the best cinematographers and the 'B' unit gets the least money.

The studio is saying, "Wait a minute, what kind of picture is this?"
He's saying, "Look, Sci-Fi is coming. We gotta make this one."
"What's Sci-Fi?" So they gave him a small budget.

Being a business, everything was a formula and each movie genre had its own specific formula. MGM was known for "carpet movies" as Western actors called them, as they were acted out in living rooms.

So besides the musicals, there were movies with great emotional depth, mysteries and intriguing international movies but they were all formulas.

Forbidden Planet was a formula movie too, but in a different way. Science fiction movies were not as well established in the mainstream at the time as a genre. Looking back from today that's hard to believe, as it seems as though at least one sci-fi movie is released very weekend.

The new literacy and experimentation during TV's Golden Age and live television forced the studios to develop different approaches to film. The writers in New York (who had nothing to lose in this new medium) would directly affect how movies would be made from then on.

Science fiction became very popular on television at that time with shows like *Space Patrol* (1950-1955) and *Captain Midnight* (1954-1958). Hollywood began to take notice—and *Forbidden Planet* was one of the results.

After the first week of shooting *Planet*, the executives upstairs, who were watching the dailies, had discovered a fine work in progress. They told him they would be giving him more money for the production.

MGM, having an "A" unit as well as a "B" unit, would send free "A" unit crew members to go and work on "B" movies like *Planet*. So the production received more attention from talents including Metro's extraordinary cameraman, George Folsey, which is why *Forbidden Planet* looked so great.

During my times at M-G-M I liked to hang out at the studio's special effects and miniature departments. The studio invested in them even while their technicians weren't working on a film, with (still) amazing results.

Planet made money like the musicals and the love stories, but what nobody knew was that it would stand the test of time and be used as a template to this day, as one of the top movies ever made. And of course, to everyone's surprise, the robot ended up becoming the big star.

I should mention that although Sci-Fi was not big in terms of the studios at the time, I actually grew up on Sci-fi through the Saturday afternoon serials.

When I would go to the movies at ten years old with my brother, we would see *Flash Gordon, Dick Tracy* and all the rest. So this was one more chance I had to live out part of a childhood dream.

Forbidden Planet just kept on going and years later, after two students who were attending at USC Film School saw it, they got busy writing science fiction. Those two students were George Lucas and Steven Spielberg.

THE TWENTY–FOUR MGM CONTRACT FILMS

1950 *A Life of Her Own* / Hosiery Man (uncredited)
1950 *The Magnificent Yankee* / Reynolds, Secretary
1951 *Grounds for Marriage* / Tommy
1951 *Cause for Alarm!* / Lonesome Sailor
1951 *Go for Broke!* / Lieutenant (uncredited)
1951 *No Questions Asked* / Detective Walter O'Bannion
1951 *Rich, Young and Pretty* / Bob Lennart
1951 *The People Against O'Hara* / Jeff Chapman
1951 *Across the Wide Missouri* / Dick
1951 *The Unknown Man* / Bob Masen
1952 *Just This Once* / Tom Winters
1952 *Scaramouche* / Philippe de Valmorin
1952 *Holiday for Sinners* / Father Victor Carducci
1952 *Fearless Fagan* / Capt. Daniels–Company J
1953 *The Story of Three Loves* / Marcel (segment "Equilibrium")
1953 *I Love Melvin* / Harry Flack
1953 *Dream Wife* / Henry Malvine
1953 *Escape from Fort Bravo* / Lt. Beecher
1953 *Give a Girl a Break* / Burton Bradshaw
1954 *The Student Prince* / Lucas
1954 *Betrayed* / John (uncredited)
1955 *Hit the Deck* / Lt. Jackson
1955 *It's a Dog's Life* / George Oakley
1956 *Forbidden Planet* / Chief Quinn

(Note: Scenes from several of Richard's MGM movies appeared in *The Metro-Goldwyn-Mayer Story* (1951), the titles of which appear below):

The Magnificent Yankee (1950), *Go For Broke!* (1951), *Rich, Young and Pretty* (1951), *Across the Wide Missouri* (1951).

Richard also appeared in the musical short *A Great Lady Has an Interview* (1954)

CHAPTER FOUR:
PATHS OF GLORY, THE FACELESS MAN & ZORRO

FROM: MCP
DATE: 3:23
You are a charismatic actor, you know, not talking much, but express so much, so well (mix of Gary Cooper/Oscar Goldman, like that), that's okay for me.

Each of your various works has been, and is, a magnificent offering to me...what a gift.

Grateful for that, more than words can ever express...

Now after seeing *Paths of Glory* here, will go see Kubrick exhibition at the French Cinematheque. It is in Paris, near Bercy, tomorrow. There's a huge picture of you in front of the theatre. Look forward to seeing you Mr. Anderson.
MCP

PATHS OF GLORY (1957) AND STANLEY KUBRICK

I was well into my fourth year at Metro-Goldwyn-Mayer when something very interesting happened. I received a call from a friend:

"There's a director wants to meet you. His name is Stanley Kubrick. "

He comes over to my apartment, sits down, and we talk about movies for three hours. He said to me "Y'know, Dick, I've seen every movie that you made when you were at MGM."

He had already made a picture, I later learned, called *The Killing* (1956). I always remember the scene where the lead character (played by Sterling Hayden) starts to leave and drops the case and money starts flying all over the airport, as the movie ends.

Later on, I received another call:

"This is Jimmy Harris, Richard. How would you like to go to Munich to make a picture?"

"Sure."

They sent me the script and I called back and said, "Yes. When do we start?"

The picture was called *Paths of Glory*.

I later learned that Stanley and his partner, James Harris, had a difficult time getting the picture made. EVERYBODY in town turned it down until finally Kirk Douglas agreed to play the major role in it. But he only did it because he was on his way to make a big picture called *The Vikings* (1958).

I'm still under contract to Metro and I have to do something about that. Metro was letting a lot of people go at this time because, in New York, Nick Schenck was looking at the numbers and saying, "You guys gotta make some moves," and they were letting some actors and actresses go at the studio. Walter Pidgeon, whom I had great respect for, said, "I'll stay here if I have to sweep the soundstages with a broom."

I asked for an appointment and I saw Benny Thaw, who ran the actors.

I said, "Benny, I'd like to have a release; there's something I want to do."

He says, "What is it?"

I said, "It's just a small movie but..."

He said, "Well, I'll go and talk..."

I said, "Benny, please. It's just a movie they'll only pay me a nickel for."

"Okay."

I arrived in Munich in the dead of winter knowing my lines, and was on the set every day because Kubrick asked me to make sure the actors knew their lines.

In those days Stanley was making some of the kind of pictures they are making today, independent releases, just all kinds of pictures that don't have studio releases. He didn't talk to me, as he had seen me in all those pictures. Stanley had an extraordinary gift in what he did with a camera.

As Maj. Saint-Aubin in *Paths of Glory*.
Photo courtesy of Richard Anderson.

COURTROOM SCENE

One day we rehearsed the courtroom scene, with my boots on the marble floor and all that inside of the castle. We had a rehearsal outside on the grass the day before with the prosecuting attorney there and the table there with the judges sitting. It was a courtroom scene.

So Stanley says "All right Richard, do the scene."

The scene is that I'm supposed to stand up and talk. I stood up and started WALKING ACROSS in front of the judges.

Stanley says "No, wait a minute, just…"

I said "Stanley, calm down."

And then he saw what I was doing. He shot it BEHIND where the judges were sitting and saw me as well.

He wanted me to come to dailies, and was all excited about the stuff. I realized then that he was all visual and it was very interesting to work that way. We had all kinds of scenes through that. We had a fine time together.

Halfway through the film he wanted me to do the court martial reading. When it came time, out comes Adolphe Menjou, George Macready, the ones to be shot, and myself. I turn, walk with the papers, turn left, then stand there facing them, saying why they are to be killed, and then we did a take.

Stanley looked at me and he says, "What are you doing?"

I said "Stanley, this is very interesting. This fellow I'm playing is a graduate of fine schools, a good person. But he's working with these generals who helped four years of death in the first World War.

He has a realization, a revelation of sorts, when he stands there to explain why they were going to die: "What am I doing?" You see it in his eyes and what I did was, you saw that I was against this, it's a short scene.

And Stanley says, "What are you doing?"

I said, "Well, that's what I was doing."

"Well, why don't you do it my way?"

So I did. I did it with a straight back, less looking at anything and just letting him have it—CUT.

The script supervisor, came over to say, "That's the one."

I said, "Will you get the ____ out of here?"

Stanley said, "Okay, I'll do it your way. But there's one thing I want to ask you..."

All right, now I have to explain that Easter was a week previous to that and I had four days off. So I took off, I went to Paris. Adolphe Menjou sent me to a good hotel. Everything went well in Paris.

Stanley, meanwhile, was talking to everybody: "How, what, when, where's Anderson?"

Someone says, "He's in Paris."

Stanley says, "You know, I saw this story in New York as a play. I did all I could to get enough money and a producer to help me make this picture. Everybody in town turned it down including Gregory Peck.

"And finally, at the last minute, we got Kirk Douglas, but he was doing it only because he was on the way to do *The Vikings*. That's the only reason he made it.

"And then we got the money from United Artists to make the picture."

He said, "All right, we'll do it your way. But you gotta do one more thing."

"'What is it?'"

"What did you do in Paris?"

I told him what he wanted to hear…With all of this stress and pressure he was under, it was probably pleasing to him vicariously. So he promised to use it my way.

That's Stanley Kubrick.

Now what happened in the end, in order to go on with the movie, they sent the script where the soldiers WERE shot to United Artists for approval. I later learned from Jimmy and Stanley that no one there had read it.

Of course, when the executives saw the completed movie, they said, "You were right."

Imagine what would have happened if he didn't like it?

We'd be back shooting again. But that's the whole movie. We all knew it wasn't a picture if the soldiers had lived. The whole point was what led up to their dying for no good reason.

Due to *Paths of Glory*, I was suddenly taken seriously as an actor in a new way, different from my Metro days.

THE BUSTER KEATON STORY (1957)

Donald O'Connor was a wonderful guy. I was Ann Blyth's lover in that movie. A very charming, nice gal. Buster Keaton came down to the set to see what was going on.

Donald says, "Come on now, Buster. Take it easy, will you? The newspaper people will kill you, because they're all over you now," because of the movie.

He was out pushing the film. And he'd come in just to say hello to Don, who would often say, "Buster, take it easy now." He was doing everything in front of the cameras all the time.

I thought it was a great honor that they made that picture for him because he was right up there. Never used a stunt man, he was incredible. I always remember *The General*. He did things like houses coming down on him.

Everybody says it was Chaplin and Lloyd, but this fellow wasn't

Photo courtesy of Richard Anderson.

far behind, and many people thought him the best.

The Buster Keaton Story also provided me the opportunity to appear in the same film as Peter Lorre, who portrayed one of the memorable characters in *Casablanca*, one of my favorite films.

Keaton was under contract at MGM when I was there. L.B. Mayer always said, "We have a family here," and was very loyal to his people. Keaton wasn't doing much, though: spent most of his time helping others.

I saw Keaton one day. About to walk into the commissary, he stopped and stared at me. I couldn't move. It was though he recognized me from working on the film, yet almost as if a reminder that such roles were no longer being offered to him.

Ironically—demonstrating what made him a master of the silent era.

KATHARINE

I met my wife through my brother who was dating a lady who he eventually married, whom he went to school with. My parents knew the family and I'd go over to their house once in a while around this period.

On one occasion, over there on the other side of the living room door was this young lady, Katharine.

I didn't know who she was so I approached her and said,

"Well, it's nice to meet you!"

She said, "You must be an actor."

I thought, "Here we go." I said, "Yes."

She said, "Well, welcome to the house."

I didn't see her for a long time after that.

To be continued…

THE LONG HOT SUMMER (1958)

I was in the company of the hottest actors in the business. Paul Newman, Joanne Woodward, Lee Remick and Orson Welles. (Coincidentally, I had just appeared with Paul and Joanne in a

Richard, Paul Newman and Joanne Woodward in *The Long Hot Summer*.
Photo courtesy of Richard Anderson.

segment of the *Playhouse 90* TV series entitled "The 80 Yard Run").

My first scene on location in Baton Rouge, Louisiana, was outside in the garden of my home. Walking down to the set, I saw Orson, who looks at me and smirks. We shot the master, medium and close shots of Joanne and Orson. My turn, no sooner did I start talking, then off-camera Orson started mumbling a low chatter. When I started my second lines, he continued.

I then did something I never did before. Put my right hand over my face. Marty Ritt, the director, called CUT. He says:

"Hey kid, what's the matter?"

"Marty, can't get the words out. Somebody's talking back there."

Off-stage, I hear Orson with those deep mellifluous tones.

"He's goddamn right."

Shot the close up then in one take. From then on, he was peaches and cream. We became friends.

Curse of the Faceless Man (1958)

One of my best known and interesting films is the low-budgeted *Curse of the Faceless Man*. I have referred to it in the past as "one I was doing on the way to something else." I've had to eat those words, somewhat, but with a good appetite, as it has turned out.

The director of the film was the prolific Edward L. Cahn, who also did many other cult films besides mainstream work such as *Law and Order* (1932) with Walter Huston, and the cult classic and *Alien* prototype *It, the Terror From Beyond Space* (1958).

Curse is essentially a contemporary remake of Boris Karloff's *The Mummy* (1932), with its themes of ancient curses, past lives, suspended animation and undying love over the centuries, with me in the David Manners role as the hero in modern day.

I got a call from William Morris saying, "They want you to do this picture but you don't want to make it.

"You just came off *Long Hot Summer* (1958) with Paul Newman and Orson Welles. It's just a little picture, an Edward Small production who has someone else's name on it instead of his own."

"I want to make it."

Small made some wonderful movies, one of the greatest of which was the original *Count of Monte Cristo* (1936) with Robert Donat.

But he would never have made it back then and did not want his name on this. It was very low budgeted. The studio was so small, there was barely enough room for me to tie my shoe!

When it was announced that the picture was going to be made, he publicly replied that he was not making it and his name will not be on it—he was angry.

What I liked about it was it had a wonderful theme. It's a love story between this man who lived in Pompeii and the girl he loved. Pompeii/Mount Vesuvius destroys him, but he comes back in a different way and he wants his lady back.

Ever since I started doing conventions I pretty well find out what's out there, what people say. They want to talk about *Curse of the Faceless Man* after it's over…more than any other.

I tell them, "I've made other pictures besides that." But they insist that they want this one. They ask me to come into the screening room after the showing to talk about it. There is at least an hour of questions.

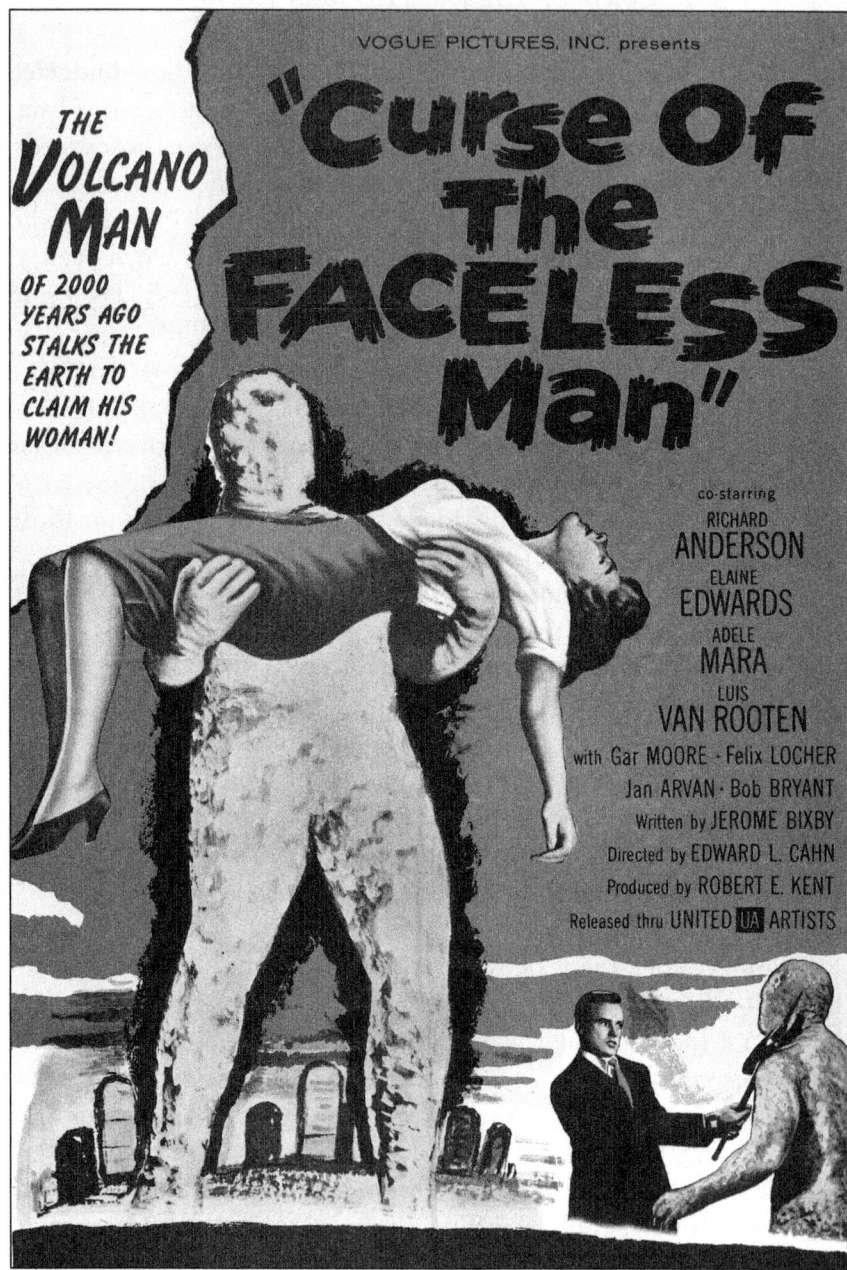

Photo courtesy of Richard Anderson.

At home, I don't screen the pictures I appeared in. It's not like a studio, it's my house! I do have art from Haiti which I visited once. The people were having terrible times but their paintings were so colorful, all about the people and the streets.

I also put up a little picture of Neil Armstrong, the first man on the moon, right by my front door as you go out. I happened to meet him shortly after it happened and he wrote something nice on it.

I mention all of this, as the only poster I have on my wall from one of the films I did was from *Curse of the Faceless Man*, as it seems to mean so much to so many people and the pleasure it's brought me in discussing it with them.

Recently, my manager, Dennis Bond, called about some business and said, "By the way, I saw a picture of yours on late night…it really got me…and you were great in it."

I said, "You don't have to tell me what it is."

He did: "*Curse of the Faceless Man*."

Mr. Bond is not one for overstating anything.

That one ought to be made again!

PERSONAL AND PROFESSIONAL ACKNOWLEDGEMENT

I first saw Curse Of The Faceless Man *when I was 12 years old. It was 1:00 in the morning on a Saturday night. I was hanging out with some friends in front of the TV in the darkened living room of my neighbor's house. We watched in fascination as this petrified stone creature suddenly comes to life and starts for a girl who for some reason was sitting in an Italian museum in the middle of the night sketching a dead body from Pompeii. The door flies open and the hero bursts in, grabs an axe and attacks the monster with it.*

This was the first time I put a name to the actor, a familiar face from countless movies and TV shows: Richard Anderson, best known as Oscar Goldman from The Six Million Dollar Man, Forbidden Planet *and* The Night Strangler.

In a strange irony, this actor who has worked with everyone from Stanley Kubrick in Paths of Glory *to a recurring role as Detective Steve Drumm on the last season of the* Perry Mason *TV series is for many most fondly remembered for his role in this little six day horror movie, a film he was once embarrassed to even admit he was in.*

His story is a fascinating one, not to mention the fact that the only movie poster he has framed on the wall of his house is from Curse Of The Faceless Man!

How times change.

I've worked in the film industry for forty years and am an avid film collector, and one of my prized acquisitions is a 16mm print of Curse Of The Faceless Man. *Thanks Richard, for all the entertainment you've provided over the years.*

MILLER DRAKE
DIRECTOR/PRODUCER/VISUAL EFFECTS EDITOR
(*Terminator 2, JFK, Green Lantern*)

CHANCE MEETING

Somewhere around this time period I saw Katharine again at a coffee shop on Wilshire Boulevard. She was sitting there reading a book.

"Oh," she says, "Hello, sit down" and we chatted.

She was married now, unfortunately, so there was nothing to pursue. We just chatted and that was it. More to come.

MY SUPPORT TEAM

I never stopped working over the years, appearing regularly on *Zorro, Perry Mason* and later *Dynasty*. Special acknowledgement to my agents for bringing all this about: Guy Steiner and Abby Gershler, William Morris and Norman Brokaw. As I mentioned earlier, success in acting, to a large degree, is dependent on how often you appear on screen, but this is probably even more the case as one gets older. With all the new faces cropping up and being sought after, it's easy to get lost in the mix.

As Ricardo del Amo in *Zorro*.
Photo courtesy of Richard Anderson.

Zorro (1957–1959)

With *Zorro*, I did two and they liked it and I came back more after that. Sometimes they'd just invite me for one show and they'd end up having me do six or seven or eight.

Guy Williams was a nice fellow, always with a big smile on his face. He didn't seem to mind me being there, although some of the supporting cast members may have felt some competition from me, whether for pay or something else, I don't know.

I had worked at all of the other studios, But Disney was different somehow. They are all there to make money of course, but with Disney it was more like a university, with an overriding higher vision that they were aspiring to.

One day I saw Walt Disney, when we were outside and he gave me a great look, having probably seen the dailies.

By the way, in a week and a half from our writing this in the Spring of 2014, I'm going to do a convention for Disney, particularly *Zorro*, what with all the fencing and the love and the dancing and the singing to the lady I was interested in from the second floor I had done on it!

Thriller: "The Purple Room" (1960)

Another fan favorite is this episode of the series *Thriller*, hosted by Boris Karloff, with whom I had the chance to share a scene at the show's introduction. I didn't get much of a chance to interact with him, but had great respect for him.

Interestingly, the episode served as a nod to several generations of Universal Studios' horror films, probably unintentionally.

Of course, Boris himself starred in films for Universal over several decades, starting with *Frankenstein* in 1931.

At a certain point in the show, I wore a mask that was used by James Cagney in *Man of a Thousand Faces* (1958) for his portrayal of Lon Chaney, the big horror star of the silent era. It was worn in a dramatization of the most famous scene from *Phantom of the Opera* (1925), one of the all-time classics.

The house set itself is best known from the Hitchcock thriller

Psycho (1960) which introduced a shocking, psychological approach to horror movies.

All of these elements came together in an episode that is well thought of by fans in its own right.

Checkmate: "The Murder Game" (1960)

This was my first job with director Douglas Heyes, who had taken a liking to me and invited me to a job in San Francisco. On the first day, they asked me to wear a blue suit, which they furnished. When I got there, out by the water, Hayes asked me to jump into the water.

He didn't tell me, but I got there and he said, "In this scene, you're having to look for something." I played a detective.

"Richard, jump in the water."

"What? What was that?"

"Jump in the water."

That started it. And I jumped in the water, and might I tell you, it's pretty cool up there!

That's how I started in a long situation with him. I was later in a picture called *Kitten With a Whip* (1964) that he did with John Forsythe. And I worked on two or three two-hour movies with him. He was extremely, extremely helpful.

Kitten With a Whip was one of the features which was famously spoofed on the *Mystery Science Theatre 3000* series.

Bus Stop (1961; not the film, but the TV series)

Based on a film of the same name with Marilyn Monroe. Got nowhere in the ratings, but I did find myself working several times with Robert Altman. I would "whistle to work" in those days. He was a terrific director. He allowed me to overlap dialogue in scenes that seemed to need a more real pace.

"Not a bad idea" he told me. Used two mikes. It was a new and learning experience, similar to that of *Long Hot Summer*.

Third Time Is the Charm

The next time I saw Katharine I had learned that she was now divorced. I was at Ray Stark's beautiful house in Bel Air where I used to go over and play tennis a lot.

One of the ladies there said that she was going to be having a big business party one evening in the summer for a picture that he would be opening the next week for which he'd hired 50 to 60 people at the house.

She walked over to me and she asked, "Would you like to come?"

"Thank you."

Then two days later she calls and says, "I have six names here and I'll read them to you."

She read the first name and I said,

"Stop!"

It was Katharine.

I picked her up that evening and she asked, "Would you like to have a drink first?"

I said, "No, let's just go to the party."

Got there and we walked towards the swimming pool which they had covered (this is Bel Air, California, folks!). They had an orchestra there and it was in the evening. People pouring, from long distance, into the house.

We sat down—the moon was just beautiful that evening and we ordered drinks.

I started to talk and this elderly woman turns to me and asks, "Will you dance with me?'

I thought "Oh, God."

But I said, "Certainly. All right." Somebody's mother, you know.

So I got up and I'm dancing with her and Katharine was just sitting there.

Finally I moved her in such a way that she ended up in her chair, which is next to me, and I have my back to her—and I looked at Katharine.

She was sitting there. She had the most beautiful eyes I've ever seen on any woman, and the moon was shining on them.

I said, "Would you like to dance?"

She says "Certainly, I'd like to."

We got up. We danced slowly and I turned in the way that I could see her face to the moon and I said "Katharine, there's something I need to tell you."

She says "Oh, what's that?"

"Looking at those beautiful eyes." I said, "I have to tell you that I love you."

She said "You really shouldn't say that to a woman. She might believe you."

And that's how it started.

She was really an interesting lady. She was a Phi Beta Kappa at college and she would tell me stories all the time, such as:

"The Chancellor asked me to come up one day. He said 'We're happy you're here. We've read about you' and so forth and so on. Is there anything you'd like?

"Uh, I'd like a place to park my car."

Everybody there just fell apart!

So we started dating and it was great fun. We did a lot of wonderful things. I asked her to marry me. She said, "Yes, I'd love to marry you."

Katharine was colorful, energetic and unpredictable, which I loved about her, and which created a vital energy between us. Yet even early on, there seemed to be a mystery present that would gradually reveal itself over time.

We were going to do something about a house down on the beach. She grew up on the beach, right there as you go down in Santa Monica. It's a beautiful house, 707. Her family had lived there.

I had put down a little to get the house, I just wanted to be certain. So we went there, we were looking at the place and suddenly she just said, "No."

I said, "What do you mean 'No'"?

"No." She got in her Porsche and drove away.

That night, I'm sitting there all by myself, wondering if putting the money down was a mistake and if it was all going to work out after all. Finally, I decided to head down to Malibu for a drink.

Along the way, I met a very kindly lady.

I asked, "Would you care to go down by where I live? We could sit out by the water."

"Oh, yes, yes!"

The Anderson Family, L to R Ashley, Deva Justine, Richard, Katharine, Brooke Dominique.
Photo courtesy of Richard Anderson.

That is pretty much what we did. Then she left and I just slept on the floor.

At about 8:00 a.m. the phone rang and it's Katharine.

"Richard?"

"Yes?"

"Where are you?"

I said, "Well, I'm at the house, in fact I slept on the floor."

"Well, what did you do yesterday?"

I said "Well, I just went out for a drink...":

"YOU WHAT?!!? You don't love me!" she said.

"Aww," I said "Katharine, of course I love you."

"I mean what, what is this?" And she started crying.

I said "Please" and we got together and it was probably the greatest time of life, of how right we were for each other.

We got a little house that we rented for the summer. We would go down there and later when our girls were older they could be on the beach all the time and they loved it. That's where she was from, and of course I enjoyed it very much.

She was really a most, most interesting lady in so many ways and we had some very good times.

CHAPTER FIVE:
PERRY MASON, THE NIGHT STRANGLER & "THE LAST FRAME"

PERRY MASON (1957–1966)

I actually worked with Raymond Burr once prior to Perry Mason in the film *A Cry in the Night* (1956). Burr played a real heavy (oh, boy, he could do heavies!), although I had very little to do with him on that one. What struck me about Burr at that time was that he was a very professional actor, as I have found all Canadian actors to be.

He could play anything and had been doing that for a long while. Raymond struck me as the kind of an actor that had covered a lot of ground around town all the time. I had heard that he was here and he was there and that he had a great "syndicate" of friends in the business: they all respected him in the highest way.

I did a pilot for a wonderful character called Arizona Ames, directed by Dick Powell for Four Star, which didn't go anywhere, because that was the year that Westerns went down.

Abe Lastfogel called me personally at William Morris and told me "We like the work, but Westerns aren't selling anymore."

The part I played was a wonderful character. They offered a role to Raymond Burr which he took immediately for me because we worked together on *A Cry in the Night*.

We talked movies, which I love to do: talking movies for hours, and he was very good at all that stuff. A very strong minded guy. *Very* strong minded.

When he heard I was doing the pilot, he came over on the first day and he said, "I'm only doing this because you're in it and I want to wish you luck." That's the kind of man he was.

With Raymond Burr and Natalie Wood in *Perry Mason*.
Photo courtesy of Richard Anderson.

Actually another cast member, William Hopper, was tested to play Perry Mason. He had the look and everything. But when you're casting something that big there are all kinds of crazy things that go on:

"Yes I like him."

"No, I don't like him."

"Somebody likes him" and so forth.

Bet you didn't know that Raymond Burr had tested for the *prosecuting attorney*.

Raymond told me the story later: "Somehow the whole thing turned around and they put me in at the last minute." This business IS the last minute! And you think Perry Mason is a solid thing, you know.

I came on to play roles in four episodes of the Mason show prior to the last year, when I then became a regular. I had gotten married by then and would be pretty busy on other things but they'd call me once in a while to do something on the show.

My reaction to the first one I played on was "Wow, this is a corporation." Everything was set to where you just came in, you went to your dressing room and you walked out. It was all very, very military in that sense, and it really worked. With that kind of rhythm, one would just fall into it in the same way.

As a guest on a series, you come and go. I was doing a lot of that too, but when one is a regular, it's really quite different. Sometimes I was asked to come back and do more episodes. That happened with me on *Twelve O'Clock High* and later on *Dynasty*. I ended up doing two seasons with them in the same part, a Westerner.

There is a big difference because, first of all, you know everybody on the set. They all know you, they see you coming and know pretty much what's going to happen. But they never worried about me very much. The crew would want to get through as early as they can, although it wasn't always that way, for which I sympathized with them: If I were a crew member, I'd think about lunch and "What time do we go home?" The hours are so long for them.

Bill Tallman, who played district attorney Hamilton Burger on *Perry Mason*, was a hell of a nice guy and had been in films for a long, long time. When he hit this one, of course, that was pay dirt in the sense of his being on all the time.

The unfortunate thing with Bill, and I so respected him for this, was the fact that although he was a heavy smoker, he was right up there. And when I joined the show, I noticed he wasn't looking well. The smoking had gotten to him, and he had cancer. But he went through the whole season with it and always had that wonderful humorous thing, saying "When am I going to win a case? "

Various guests would appear on the series, one of whom was Brian Donlevy, in the episode "The Case of the Positive Negative."

He says, "C'mon, let's have lunch." So we went across the street to where I'd always had lunch while I was on the *Mason* series. This guy went to the U.S. Naval Academy at Annapolis, was a military man. He went over to Paramount, was one of the guys that Preston Sturges picked out, and made all these pictures with him (for those who don't know, Sturges was one of the great writer/directors of the last century).

Also, his dressing room was right near that of Bill Holden, with whom he was great friends. One thing he told me which I'll never forget was that when Donlevy left Paramount, he called up Holden and said "Holden, get over here. Get over here now. Get your stuff and put it in my dressing room before I leave."

Bill Holden had told me that it was one of the great dressing rooms. Donlevy told all kinds of stories about his life and military experiences and these were kind of his last days.

It's very interesting in the business—when you're working and lunch comes, and you hear about some of the people that you saw when you grew up.

They would hire a lot of actors who didn't work much, and wanted them on the show to keep them going and so forth and Donlevy was just guesting in a few things. He was in *A Cry in the Night* as well. Edmond O'Brien was on that movie too and he did some scenes with Donlevy and they had their time "one upping" each other.

They would hire a great many actors who were very, very well known in their career. Another one who was in the very first episode I did was Robert Armstrong who, as Carl Denham in the original *King Kong* (1933), had the classic movie line "'Twas beauty killed the beast." But the problem was that you never had time to talk to them, as you were busy.

Raymond Burr was always very busy in his trailer; one didn't see him much. You could see he had sort of a high table and he'd be there, where he'd read the scripts. In other words, he didn't depend on teleprompters in that sense. The first year, he did it without teleprompters. But then on, it was just impossible with the amount of dialogue he had. It was "making him old fast." So when I'd see him on the occasional times that I'd work, he was off in the corner learning about the story.

It was on the ninth and last year that I was invited to play Lt. Steve Drumm, the police element for the whole season.

It was fun working on *Perry Mason*. Raymond could have written a book of jokes. He always had something going on to keep things light, to bring some humor to it. Barbara Hale would organize the parties; when someone wanted to talk with Ray, even if it had been the front office, they would go to Barbara as go-between and say, "Listen, we've got thus and such about, you know…" about whatever it was.

ERLE STANLEY GARDNER

It's the last day of the show. They were having a party, everyone was having a good time. We were eating a little food; I was sitting where I worked and was having a drink.

The actor playing the judge says, "Oh, Mr. Anderson, I'd like to talk to you for a minute."

So I turned to the person I was talking to and I said, "There's so many judges that come here all the time and I don't even remember who he is."

I walk over and say, "Well, it's quite a day, isn't it?"

Then he says, "Yes. I wanted to tell you how much I enjoyed working with you and I just want to give you a compliment on how much I enjoyed the way you were playing Lieutenant Steve Drumm."

I said "Thank you, thank you very much."

I thought he was just an actor complimenting another actor.

He reaches out his hand and I remember when he said it, I almost fell over:

"I'm Erle Stanley Gardner."

Now, let's get a reaction here: I shook hands with him and I said: "Wow!"

I had a very good time. We were having children and it was easy because all I do is drive down there and I don't have to work all day sometimes. The courtroom scenes were full days and I'd testify in the courtrooms.

But the whole thing about a show like that is, it could have run like *Gunsmoke*. Could have run 20 years, 30 years. But when I got on it, I was settling into what I thought would be, who knows? What happened was that the Chairman of CBS William Paley got into negotiations with producer Gail Patrick about going to color.

Gail was producer as well as actress and was married to an advertising man, Thomas Cornwell Jackson, a very nice man and a powerful man. However, for some reason, they couldn't get to the numbers, and cancelled the show. William Paley called and said, "I regret this happened. It had to do with numbers. But I want you to know it was the one show I watched every Sunday night." So it gives you an idea of how powerful it was.

If you really want to talk about a series that had longevity, particularly in the minds of viewers, it was the *Six Million Dollar Man*. I see it in the headlines: A "Six Million Dollar" whatever, a six million dollar package, a six million dollar airplane or whatever it is. Perry Mason was always "Who do you think you are, Perry Mason?" It had that "trademark."

It's fun.

It's hard to remember a favorite episode, but I'll tell you, the parts they gave me before I was a regular were always fun. They were full of stuff. Full of all kinds of Machinations. Drumm was a straight guy, I played him straight. He was the kind of guy that was investigative and was pretty much having to do with "No, she was not in the bathroom the day that so and so was shot," that kind of stuff. "I found a ring with her initials on the inside, and it was in her car. It wasn't her car, though, it was the man who was killed..." It was a very good part. I got a lot of work from it.

Senior Turner Classic Movies Researcher Alexa Foreman is a wonderful, wonderful lady. She's been sending me stuff through my Metro connection there (Turner owns the MGM library), such as all 24 pictures that I did at MGM. I called her one day a number of years ago about a film book that was coming out, to find out if she knew anything about it.

She said "Oh, Mr. Anderson." She said "Yes, we have a book here, by the way, we've got a spare copy…My God, you're on television!"

I said "Really?"

She says "*Perry Mason*."

Turner Classic Movies Senior Researcher

Normally I have my TV on TCM (we all have TVs here) but I had switched over to Perry Mason *which I love, and there was Richard on the screen as Detective Drumm, and the phone rang and it WAS Richard.*

It was great. I've known Richard since 1998 and I consider him a true friend and a wealth of information. —Alexa Foreman.[1]

THE FUGITIVE (1963–1967)

I did a lot of work on *The Fugitive*.

Before *The Fugitive* went off the air it was announced that they were going to reveal who it was who killed Richard Kimball's wife. On the last night, the whole country was making a bet on who the killer was, and the Vegas money was that the brother-in-law was the guy who did it.

Well, when it came out, it WASN'T him. I played the role of the brother-in-law and I was a little worried!

There was a lot of money lost on that show. Seventy two percent of America watched that segment at that time. But that was a very high number. A lot of night shooting.

David Janssen, by the way, had a great sense of humor. Fun. Quinn Martin let it be known that he would never make a show with just one character again because it wore him. And it was really tough on David, because he was in every scene. It's extremely hard.

I was working on a show that took place at night, and we gathered a big crowd. David wasn't there, and I had a scene to do. And when I came out, the audience just burst into APPLAUSE.

I found out later that David did something that was unlike him, really, but right after that HE had to come out. And he got, I must say, tumultuous applause.

But I thought that was kind of cute, because he always used to say, "I'm doing this to get rich." He was all worn out after *Fugitive*. He did one more show after that with Jack Webb. I enjoyed working with him. He made it so easy.

12 O' CLOCK HIGH (1964–1967)

I did one segment of it, and was actually in the original movie, which was my first job. I got the role and went down to Florida and waited two weeks just to be an American aviator that comes out of an airplane not too well. One day shooting, but I was there. It was a Gregory Peck movie.

They asked me to come and do *12 O'Clock High* as a series. So I did one of them. There was another role of an officer who was going after things that he wanted done and they wanted me to come back like I had done on other shows. But unfortunately—or fortunately, however it would be—I was invited back.

THE GREEN HORNET (1966)

I have been asked about working with Bruce Lee on *The Green Hornet*. He was just a nice guy, that's all. We didn't have much contact on *The Green Hornet*.

It's just amazing, though, the mail I get on that show. It was very popular with some. I knew a couple of actors who would say "Gee, I hope we quit early. I want to get home to see *The Green Hornet*."

That was a wonderful kind of series, with the cars and all that, a very fine show. I liked to play gangsters, as I did here.

I also played a gangster on *The Untouchables*, which was another big show. I knew Robert Stack fairly well; he was a funny guy, had a great sense of humor. Played the part well, I thought.

The director for the *Hornet* episodes was William Beaudine, a prolific director from the silent days on, who was nicknamed "One Shot" for his proficiency in completing a film quickly and efficiently. He had done several hundred movies and TV shows in his career—he was very organized.

William Dozier, who was the Executive Producer of the show, also did the phenomenally successful *Batman* TV series just prior to this. On *Perry Mason*, Billy Hopper would say every week "Gee, I hope I finish, I want to see *Batman*." That was a sensation.

DAN AUGUST (1970–1971)

With Burt Reynolds for Quinn Martin Productions. We had one year of it. It was going very well. Quinn Martin was doing it. He was a very well-known man. I had been appearing as a guest star often on other shows that he was producing such as *The Fugitive, The FBI*, etc.

Burt was fun. He was generous in the works. An actor who had a winning way about him that led him on to becoming hot. By the way, part Native American. We still communicate.

More later, but he helped me by appearing in videos for an organization that I am still involved with: The California Indian Manpower Consortium (A federally funded organization to help educate young people in the eighty California tribes.

We had it all worked out and suddenly some other show just came in, not a big show, but a comedy, and it just knocked us out. How's this for a bit of irony: ABC cancelled it but then CBS picked it up two summers later, and it then became the hit of the off-season!

Burt was quite a guy. He was a lot of fun.

SECONDS (1966), *THE NIGHT STRANGLER* (1973) AND "THE LAST FRAME"

I was once told, "Richard, the best thing an actor can have in a movie is to be in the last frame of it. People will remember you."

That happened in two places: It happened in *Seconds* and it also happened in a two-hour TV movie I did called *The Night Strangler*.

In *Seconds*, I was the physician who operated on Rock Hudson and it was really a story about a man who wants to be younger: He's an older man, and I'm the surgeon who makes him younger, and he turns out to be Rock Hudson.

There was a little shot where Hudson was all alone and he's thinking about when he was younger—the idea was that when he was a older man he should have stayed that way, with his children and everything, but now it was too late.

But I had the last line in that one. In the end I have to put him away because he knows too much. We have to do that because they start talking about you, so they have me cut him up and saying good-bye to him. Then they just take him away and he's dead now and I say "Hmm. Too bad. He was my favorite patient."

OUT!

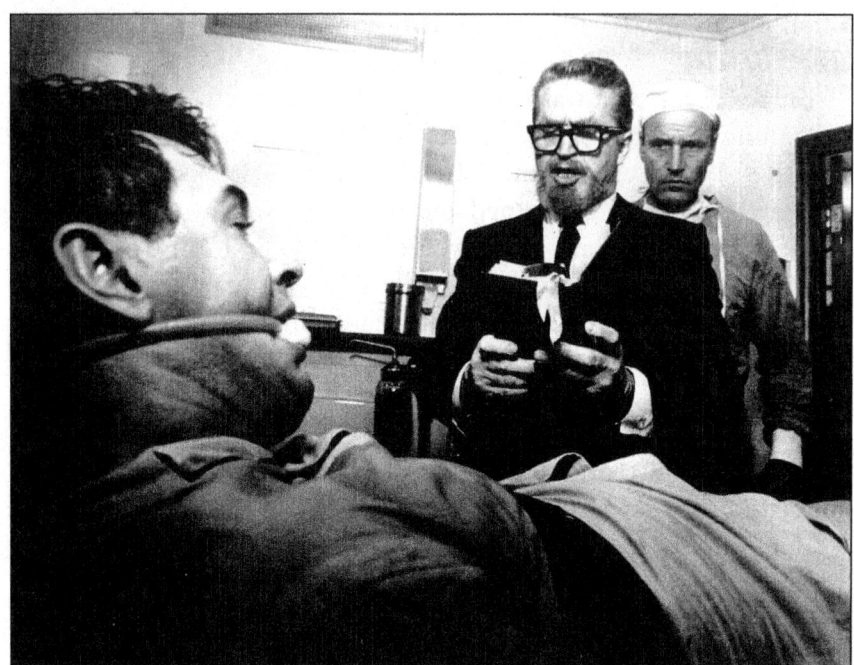

With Rock Hudson in *Seconds*.
Photo courtesy of Richard Anderson.

The inspiration for *The Night Strangler* was the Underground City in Seattle, Washington. Richard Matheson saw it and came up with the idea of a vampiric character who had been a surgeon in the Union Army during the Civil War who now needed blood like Dracula, and so terrorized the city since 1889. It was shot at the Bradbury Building on Broadway in Los Angeles, with the final sequences being done in a huge mansion down in Santa Monica, with everything lit darkly. At the end, it's there that he comes to find another lady victim.

Darren McGavin, who played the investigative reporter, was trying to save the lady. Finally the doctor realizes his time has come. He can't get any more and you see him transform into his actual age. I had the best moment at that point when suddenly you see me as a 100 year old man, turn to the detective, say so long, wave and jump out of a window!

End of movie, last shot.

And of course, at the end of the credits there was a picture of me!

It was a top-rated show at the time. Years and years later, fans remember the film, but I have a feeling it had something to do with that last scene in there.

William Tuttle, who was the makeup man at Metro for many years, had succeeded Jack Dawn and was at Metro through my time and beyond that. He came and did the makeup on it.

Putting the makeup on me was a long one. That was a big job which took several hours. Tuttle was good to the end. He'd still do jobs once in a while.

I had been trying to find a picture from that. Finally, someone brought one in. I signed it and I said, "Do you mind throwing it away?"

THE NEW PERRY MASON: "THE CASE OF THE TELLTALE TRUNK" (1973)

Monte Markham as Perry Mason.

We shot that in Canada. Two things I can tell you about that. Keenan Wynn was in the one that I was in, and he was wonderful. Keenan Wynn was at Metro all those years, and a splendid actor. In fact, Kubrick hired him for *Dr. Strangelove* (1964). Stanley once mentioned Keenan's name and said, "You know, he's a very good actor and I saw him with you on that."

The interesting thing about Monte Markham was that he NEVER blew a line. He was incredible. He was always ready. He had it all right. I remember that Keenan would try a lot of things and in trying a lot of things, you have to take time with them, because sometimes it wouldn't work, sometimes it would.

Making choices is what you do when you act. Monte Markham was absolutely, absolutely a robot. He could just do the scene, long scenes and all of that. And Keenan was being interrogated once and he had to do it two or three times, and then he heard Monte do it, the speeches, and then Monte walked away, leaving Keenan flustered. Their approaches didn't match, a problem that often occurs between actors.

It only ran a year.

Separation

Around this time, about eleven years into our marriage, Katharine and I had already begun to go our separate ways. She was bringing up the children and I was working a lot and she finally came to me and said "I think we have to make some changes here."

She said "My brother lives in Aspen and, as you know, all I ever wanted in life is a bookstore and I don't want to do it here"—we had some friends who had already set up their own bookstore in West L.A. but which wasn't the kind of arrangement that she wanted. So we made changes.

I asked her if I could keep the house, to just hang on to it, if they were to come back at some point, and she said "Sure, that's no problem."

We divorced in 1973.

She then found a small house there and moved to Aspen. Of course I went up to visit from time to time. Landing in Aspen in those days with just those prop planes was enough to get one killed, but I did go up a lot.

Then finally she found a house right near where the best hotel is and she opened up her bookstore. I came out and bought some books and she was very happy with all of that.

Then the children were having problems so she asked me to take two of them to live with me, so they moved out to the house. The third one stayed until she graduated.

But what she did that was so interesting was this: Aspen was really growing now and there were a lot of things that were being thought about. For example they talked about animal rights there, or "fur fight" as it was referred to.

She had the bookstore in very good shape by now as well as a little restaurant on top of it. Everybody was going there and the books I used to see were the best of their kind. She also had a private office and not too many people went in there—she alone wanted that. But she had developed an interest in animal rights and that there are a lot of animals there which she said should not be killed.

I said "Well, in what way?"

"Well, we shouldn't wear fur," that's all she said.

So the town sort of heard this and then at the airports all the kids who loved the idea went over and they said "You shouldn't wear fur anymore" and they really helped. I'm sure everyone who is reading this knows it was that way back then.

There was this one lady, one morning comes out a little tired, it's a tough landing and everything, and she had on a fur coat from her knees to her ears and they said "How could you do such a thing like that?"

She said, "Do you know how many men I had to ____ to get it?"

The place went up in smoke! And of course one of the last and best was her.

It was actually the traps that Katherine was after. They were such that the animals lived on for three or four days afterwards and so eventually the whole country set up a law that you had to use a certain kind of trap. That was the first.

I know now what it was with her: she wanted to be somebody. That's the reason for the change, what it was about.

And the second thing was the banning of smoking indoors because she smoked all her life and by gosh that went in the country, today there is no smoking in the bars. It was Katherine, you see. So I think she felt like she really came through.

CHAPTER SIX:
"WE HAVE THE TECHNOLOGY."

THE SIX MILLION DOLLAR MAN (1974–1978)

Not long after my separation from Katharine I received a call from one of my agents, Guy Steiner. He says "Universal Studios offered you a role in a new series called *The Six Million Dollar Man*."

"*Six Million Dollar Man*? What do they want me to do?"

"They just want you."

My family had just moved to Aspen, Colorado to live. I read the script, as well as Martin Caidin's book *Cyborg*, upon which it was based. I got all the terms of the contract and wardrobe fittings completed and showed up on time the first day of shooting, which was a hospital scene with Lee, who was in the bed, ready, by the way. Lee and I always arrived early.

I hadn't much sleep the night before and not much a week before that, bleary-eyed but grateful for the turn of work and I slipped on a pair of dark glasses.

The next day I came into work, the producer came down—in other words, "Watch out."

He said "Richard, ABC saw you and you're perfect for the part and you LOOK GREAT!"

I thanked the dark glasses! The two-hour movie went through the roof in ratings. Glenn Larson, the producer at the time, came into my trailer to tell me we were going to series, Friday night, eight o'clock.

Steve and Oscar: Who was that other "Dynamic Duo?"
Photo courtesy of Richard Anderson.

LEE MAJORS

Although Lee has the big, handsome and rugged persona that comes across as a first impression, he is also one of the brightest, quickest and smartest people that I've ever known. Besides that, he is modest and unassuming and a natural talent. Similar to Gary Cooper—high praise if you've read so far. He even appeared in the sequel to *High Noon*!

The contact between Lee and myself during the show was actually more of a social and personal nature, discussing sports and going out for a beer. We never went into great depth about the characters and their relationship. The way we worked it was when his lips stopped moving, that was my cue to talk and when mine stopped, that was his cue to start.

The focus of the show was action and the purpose of the characters was to provide a framework and a lead-in to that, so that it became kind of a shorthand to that goal—with some fun along the way.

The Intro

Shortly after working hard one night, I got a call from the producer, Harve Bennett, who asked me to come around and do some off-camera stuff. He called me in the morning and it was dark by the time I was leaving. I just about went through the gates: "Oh my God, I forgot"

So I went back into the screening room and there he was waiting. I said, "I'm sorry."

He said "It's all right Richard, just, just do this one…":

> Steve Austin: Astronaut.
> Barely alive.
> We can make him better than he was.
> Better, faster, stronger.
> We've got the technology.

And that's been playing all over the world for all these years.

Everybody who sees me says it, talks about it and says it all the time: The best intro ever done.

Shortly after that I learned that when they were editing one night, one of the editors had hit the wrong button in an action scene and in the scene, Lee Majors was running around half-speed. That opened up an action sequence like none other, that had ever been seen in an action show.

The morning after the first showing on the air at ABC, the next day my three daughters called me from school and said with giggling: "Daddy, everyone is running around in slow motion!"

From Charlton Comics' *The Six Million Dollar Man* comic book series. Note the slow motion visual effect reproduced for the comic page.
Graphic courtesy of Richard Anderson. Art by Joe Staton.

Farrah Fawcett

Lee got married to Farrah Fawcett, who then appeared in four episodes the show. In one of them she had a little scene to say with me. She was a little further back and then she said her line:

"Well, you know Oscar, did it *physically* happen…?"

I said "Farrah, I'll tell you about that…"

That place went up in smoke!

Lee just came over and he says, "What are you doin' with my wife?"

The Bionic Woman (1976–1978)

Toward the end of the first year, I'd been saying it, "Why don't we get a lady on the show?" In those days it was just two men. So it was decided (I'm not saying I was the one who got it settled) that they would look for somebody.

A lot of people auditioned, including a lady named Lindsay Wagner, who had just been dropped from the studio. They said that she didn't have the stuff and they were suggesting one or two other people, but Fred Silverman over at ABC said, "You guys don't understand—this is the lady."

It was so embarrassing to the studio to have dropped her…she's making $100 a week or whatever, but they dropped her and she gets the part and it's great.

On the first day of shooting with her, two things: First of all, it was up north and she's a tennis player on the court and she couldn't hit a thing. I went over there and I slowed her up. I said, "All you have to do is this." I drew back and said, "Do this."

POW!

"That's how to do it!" And that did it.

Lee just says it. And he says it as a very good athlete, and it works, you see. Now the first scene I had with Lindsay, we were sitting outside somewhere and it was a short scene. I was just looking out and away and she was sitting sort of next to me, a little distance away.

She said her first line. I said, "Wow, we're gonna have some fun here!" She was playing the whole thing great, great. A smile on her face, saying "Come on, let's have some fun here!" That's what created it. I treated her differently in the shows, which was very effective.

Lindsay was trying to do less of war and killings and things like that and succeeded to some degree. That was a very, very fine, perfect job of casting. The three of us got on very well.

So that was very much what happened and it was successful and of course sometimes they played together.

"Before we said goodbye to Richard Anderson and watched him drive off in his expensive and beautiful new car, we had to ask a personal question about the character he plays.

'Is Oscar Goldman in love with Jaime Sommers?'

'Yes, he is," Anderson answered without hesitation.

'It's not in the script, and we never talked about it—but it just sort of happened. I guess Oscar couldn't help himself."[1]

LINDSAY WAGNER

The Bionic Woman was really a lot of fun. Lee's was good, too, but his was much different. His show was all guy's stuff. But Lindsay had a masseuse on the set for people that needed massages, to have their backs massaged. There was no reason not to, owing to the number of hours that we were all working.

She was always for having fun on the set if possible, though the hours were just killing everybody. In those days, Lindsay wasn't up to it, in energy. But she is now, she's really amazing. She was the first woman who was running her own show, so to speak.

It had turned out that it took more days than when a man did it. I'm not saying that it is today, but in those days that's how it was.

THE FLOCK

The writer wrote a sequence in *The Bionic Woman* where Lindsay Wagner had been kidnapped and I set out to get her and we find out where it is. So we go to this place and I've got about four guys with me. She's in that building over there and it turns out there's

Oscar and Jaime.
Photo courtesy of Richard Anderson.

some nuns nearby too. Just as we start to go a whole flock of sheep cross the road. So Kenny Johnson, who was writing most of the dialogue, said:

"There's a line here I want you to say."

"All right."

So when the sheep cross the road, I say, "Get the flock out of here."

I said "Kenny, what in the hell, you're not...?"

And he got it through!

The mandatory *Mad* Magazine and *Cracked* Magazine satires.
Art by John Severin and Mort Drucker.
Graphics courtesy of Richard Anderson.

DRYDEES: THE DISPOSABLE DIAPER

Although the exact time period is uncertain (I think it was sometime after *Paths of Glory* but before *Six Million Dollar Man*) my agents arranged for me to do a commercial, so I went in to do it. I didn't know what it was until I was handed a script. Tag line: "Drydees: the disposable diaper that helps keep your baby dryer." And so I did it.

I thought there'd be some comedy in this. And there certainly was. What else could it be? It was Procter and Gamble. Next thing I know, I'm out in Malibu, three locations.

I go down to the beach and I see twelve pair of blue suits. The cameraman had a lift, high on a crane, and then we're just going to roll alongside of where the water is and we'll shoot, probably in a half an hour.

We're going to talk about "Drydees, the disposable diaper that helps keep your baby dryer."

We started shooting late morning, and we shot all day long. We must have shot fifteen or twenty times, but each time the surf kept coming in. So by the tenth or twelfth take, I suddenly see in peripheral vision, the waves are getting higher and higher, all the while the director is speaking down to me on the boom.

On the twelfth take, well, you know that wave hit me like a *rock*. I couldn't handle that and I fell down—still talking.

We did about ten others after that, changing suits every time, and left when the sun went down. This was a three-day shoot.

So, next day, I went to the Warner Bros. Ranch (all the studios had ranches around then). They had me sitting in a horse trough, telling the story, saying "Drydees, the disposable diaper that helps keep your baby dryer."

We went to Pasadena, to the fountains at the City Hall, and found myself sitting in the fountains, doing one hundred takes…quite a number anyway.

The actual diapers were made in Germany. However, they sent the diapers to be made in Germany and it turns out something went wrong with the material and so the commercials never got on the air. But that is not the end of the Drydees saga…

To finish this story, one time in the first year of *Bionic Woman* they were showing show bloopers of people messing a line, or saying

"Oh, nuts" or "Aw, come on, It's getting late, the sun's going down." "Can we do this scene..." or saying *other* words as well (I talk a lot...). That kind of stuff can be really funny.

I'm sitting there and suddenly I hear, "Drydees, the disposable diaper that helps make your baby dryer" and I look up, and there it was and the place goes up in smoke. And LINDSAY is roaring with laughter, and THERE I am!

She comes over and she makes this great remark, she says, "You know, Richard, if this thing had sold and gone on TV, it would have been the end of your career."

"Lindsay," I said, "I think if that had gone on the air would have been the beginning of my career in comedy!"

Still not over yet...more Drydees fodder.

I was on an airplane once, on my way east, and one of the attendants came over to me and she said:

"Mr. Anderson, I want to tell you I've always admired your work...'

Six Mill was on the air, getting a lot of mail, etc.

THEN:

"...Particularly on the Drydees commercial."

"*What* are you talking about?"

She said "We got it and we used to run it on all the airplanes."

"So they're running the Drydees commercial?"

She says "Yes!"

I said it very loud:

"I'M GONNA SUE THEM!"

PRODUCER OF THREE BIONIC TV MOVIES

We did three two-hour TV movies: *The Return of the Six-Million-Dollar Man and the Bionic Woman* (1987), *Bionic Showdown: The Six Million Dollar Man and the Bionic Woman* (1989) and *Bionic Ever After?* (1994), which I also produced. I sold the studio on the idea which was mine, not theirs, and then they made me go to the networks to sell it. I didn't have any sponsor; that's how it works in television. Over a period of seven years we did three of them, all highly rated.

With a bionic Sandy Bullock in *Bionic Showdown*...
Photo courtesy of Richard Anderson.

Bionic Showdown...was one of the very first films of future A-lister Sandra Bullock.

Then I came back and wanted to do the movie reboot. They gave me the okay, but the license for Martin Caidin's book had expired and needed to be renewed: he had passed away two months prior and the daughters wanted some remuneration. I won't go into all the details with the studios and so forth, but they didn't come up with much. But...

They went into negotiations with Universal and Miramax offered them a LOT of money. Now they have the rights. And I get all kinds of mail about this...

"Is there going to be a movie?"

Happily at this writing a reboot of the series is finally underway with Mark Wahlberg in the role of Steve Austin. However this time it will be *The Six Billion Dollar Man,* adjusted for today's inflation. Release is scheduled for 2016 by Dimension Films.

BIONIC WOMAN (2007 TV SERIES)

I was not the producer for this one nor did I appear in it. It followed the dark/down and dirty formula which has been adhered to in practically all superhero genre shows for some years now.

Remakes don't always work. It had a huge first night. Of course it beat everything because everybody in the audience was hoping to see what they had seen before...which is a positive show.

The problem with it really was that this one was cold. It was violent and it was mean spirited and very dark. It was no fun. Do you know who said that? *L. A. Times* writer Mary McNamara. In a review just before it went on the air she wrote "I miss Oscar (Goldman)...As played by Richard Anderson, Oscar lent a paternal heart to that '70s (version)."[2] Some of the things that I had hoped would happen in the development of that role, that is, for him to be really seriously for the country and loyal to his employees with some thought behind it weren't in there.

COZI

When I started working on *SMDM*, there was a producer who said something I'll never forget. He said "Richard, your recognition will be like no other recognition in any other form, including motion pictures. You will be seen more, and you will be known more, by them."

qui est richard anderson?

"Dans "La Femme Bionique" et "L'Homme de $6 Millions, c'est Richard Anderson qui tient ce fameux rôle d'Oscar Goldman."

The International renown of Richard Anderson.
Graphic courtesy of Richard Anderson.

"Why?"

"Because in a series, in this case, it was on for five years. You have a hundred, five hundred, six hundred films they start playing over and over again."

Currently, these many years later, they are back on television on Cozi, an offshoot of NBC: Tuesday night, *The Bionic Woman* and Wednesday, *The Six Million Dollar Man*. It is a most extraordinary happening, where today it is playing all over the world, including through Netflix, DVD and cable TV

It means that you're getting people to watch, and new people all the time. *The Six Million Dollar Man* and *The Bionic Woman* are syndicated all over the world, like few series in the history of television. It is now starting to play in the Ukraine, Lithuania and China!

SPECIAL ACKNOWLEDGMENT

In the film business, it's funny: you work and you see people in close experiences in front of the camera for long periods of time…and then years can go by without a trace of them.

Not long after the success of *Six Million Dollar Man*, Cary Grant called one day and asked if I'd like to come out to Hollywood Park with my three daughters, Ashley, Brooke and Deva on a Saturday, as he was a Board member there. He would invite friends to come out and "bet two dollars." That's what he would say! "Two dollars."

Cover courtesy of Richard Anderson.

As we headed up to the private area where we watched the horses run, people kept coming up to me for autographs, mentioning *SMDM* and other film and TV shows I had been on. I tell you, the private area is just unbelievable with the food and drinks (when you were on the board at Hollywood Racetrack in those days) and the whole ambiance of the place was important and the girls had a very good time. Cary had his daughter with him, too.

But that's when he learned, because I hadn't seen him in many, many years and he had remarried and I had remarried and all that and I hadn't seen him. And then later on when this happened he was just reacquainting, just across the way from me was where he lived and he wanted to have lunch with my daughters and me.

When we sat down to order with some of his other friends, Cary turned to me and my daughters and said:

"Betsy, my then-wife discovered your father on a TV show. She asked me to look and see what you did. I looked and agreed. It was just wonderful and we rather got him started.

"He was doing some wonderful comedy stuff. Now listen, at my age, when you see a young man, doing that well at comedy, we said 'Absolutely, let's just do something' and we got him started."

He then turned to me and said:

"Richard, I am so proud of you. You made it."

CHAPTER SEVEN:
THE POST-"BIONIC" YEARS

DYNASTY (1981–1989)

On the *Dynasty* TV series I played the semi-alcoholic Senator Buck Falmont who had a prominent role in several of the cliffhanging developments in the series, one of which concerned whether I was really the father of young Clay (played by Ted McGinley).

We would receive the scripts for the show just three days before we began shooting the episodes. All of the pages were stamped "CONFIDENTIAL," reminiscent of the many CIA types I've played over the years!

COVER UP (1984–1985)

I had finished a year on another series called *Cover Up* with Jennifer O'Neill at Fox Studios. There was a very heart-rending accident that occurred. The leading man, Jon-Erik Hexum accidentally shot and killed himself. It was on a Saturday morning and I had just left the studio.

What happened actually was that he was playing with one of the guns that morning. He had turned it towards himself and it fired and hit him in the head.

The show lasted a year. We had another actor doing it and it was dropped after that. It was very well liked.

One thing that came after was that the film business got around to all of the special effects people to eliminate all guns. It was a terrible thing. He was a very nice and extremely bright guy.

I went down to see him but he was already unconscious, and I was unable to talk to him. It was very unfortunate and sad.

PERRY MASON RETURNS (1985)

I had a wonderful part. Really a great, great part.

It was just kind of fun on the first day I saw Raymond. He was an amazing guy. He had a little scripture out in front of the dressing room. It just had four words; I wish I could think of it now, it's been a long time. And he had a younger fellow playing the police part:

"Richard, hello."

"Hello, Raymond, how are you kid?"

"Fine. We have a 'young Richard Anderson' playing your part." You know what I said?

"What's the matter with the 'old' one?!"

We'd joke back and forth. I went to his memorial out of respect for his excellence in work. And the whole world was there. They were all there, the actors and directors and producers.

KIPLINGER WASHINGTON NEWSLETTER

Starting in 1984, I was invited to do a commercial called the *Kiplinger Washington Newsletter* for fifteen years as spokesman. It is a Washington newsletter that covered business as well as international affairs and has been around since 1923.

Austin Kiplinger Sr., who was the one who started it, was a wealthy man and ended up owning a lot of land in Washington D.C. Austin Kiplinger, Jr. is the gentleman running it now. It's not a big company, but they have maybe 340,000 subscribers, possibly a million. It's all about money.

And it turns out the fellow who represented me out here, Robert Day, was trying to find somebody for the job. And he was at home one day and he says "Does anybody know anything about a guy that can do this?'

The son said "Well, get Richard Anderson. He's the Washington man on *The Six Million Dollar Man*."

So that's how I started.

We would shoot mostly in La Jolla, and we'd always have a wonderful time on our days off. Bob Day would have a representative from the company and it was just fun. A lot of hard work, but a lot of fun, too.

It's not on the air now because they only offered it on cable, and it got to be too expensive. That's the only reason it stopped. We shot it in Hong Kong once.

They would also send out notices about *The Kiplinger Washington Newsletter* and would always send me a copy, up until several years ago. I still send for them.

But when I was in Washington, I spoke to the current concern, to meet everybody, mainly business people. Kiplinger Washington Newsletter was a very fine association, and though you don't hear too much about it they're very much involved today.

We were able to open it up to other people.

When I talked to the gentleman that runs it now, one of his sons, he said, "Everyone thought you were Austin Kiplinger." It was just a very fine account.

I remember I was at a party also at the race track. Cary Grant invited me to come with my lady friend, with his wife and some of his friends. He had Gregory Peck there as well and he brought his wife and his mother.

She was sitting there with us and she said that I seemed familiar to her.

Gregory said "Yes, he's done TV and film."

She says "No, something about business. "He was on *The Kiplinger Washington Newsletter,* wasn't he?"

Of all things. Well, these things happen.

KNIGHT KIPLINGER ON RICHARD ANDERSON

The Kiplinger magazine was, in 1952, the first magazine ever to sell subscriptions on the new medium of television, when it became the first advertiser on NBC's bold experiment in early-morning TV

Sometime in the 1980s, Kiplinger went looking for a new on-air talent to do its TV spots for The Kiplinger Letter, and someone—perhaps our

LA-based advertising consultant and media buyer, Bob Day—suggested the respected veteran Hollywood actor Richard Anderson. Richard was well-known to TV audiences of the 1970s for his portrayal of a CIA officer in two hit series, The Six Million Dollar Man and The Bionic Woman, and he also did corporate advertising for Shell Oil in the late '70s and early '80s, as the "Shell Answer Man." When the execs at Kiplinger looked at his audition tapes, they saw the perfect persona to sell The Kiplinger Letter…an authoritative, serious, yet friendly manner, from an actor who looked and sounded like a real business executive…the sort of person who would read the Letter.

Kiplinger signed Anderson to a contract around 1984, and he continued to do the publisher's Letter commercials for the next 10 or so years, into the mid-1990s. Most aired on CNN, but also on other cable networks. The Kiplinger Letter spots featuring Anderson in the 1980s were a highly successful sales technique for the company, accounting for almost one-third of its total annual new-subscription sales in a given year.

In the commercials, Anderson sat or stood at a desk in an executive office setting, wearing a fine suit and tie, performing a script (read from a Teleprompter) extolling the benefits of reading The Kiplinger Letter. He seemed knowledgeable, believable, and sincere, with just the right air of gravitas.

At Kiplinger, senior executives like Knight Kiplinger, editor in chief and chairman, and his father, Austin Kiplinger, editor emeritus, remember the company's long relationship with Richard Anderson with great respect and fondness. "Richard has always been a class act…professional, well-prepared, authoritative, and highly personable, both on screen and off," recalls Knight Kiplinger." We always looked forward to having lunch with him either in LA or when he occasionally visited us in Washington. He was, and is, a consummate gentleman—even sending hand-written 'thank-you' notes and holiday greetings on his elegant monogrammed note cards. It was an honor to have had him on our team at Kiplinger."

KNIGHT KIPLINGER
EDITOR IN CHIEF AND PRESIDENT
The Kiplinger Letter, Kiplinger's Personal Finance, and *Kiplinger.com*[1]

I did other commercials too. I did one in Alaska for a bank. It was successful, but people kept writing in "What do you have a person from the United States doing a commercial about Alaska for?" Doesn't that sound like Alaska? That's the way they are up there. You know, they like their land, they don't want anybody to come up there.

We could talk about Alaska further, but I don't think we will. But they like it the way it is, and stay away! There are more airplanes in Alaska than anyplace in the world, because they all have their own airplanes.

THE *STRAIGHT* STORY

There are a lot of stories out there that are told, but some of them just aren't true. I would say this: sometimes they're told by people in our business that are much older, and they want to be interviewed. I have found, in listening to some of these stories, that they tend to exaggerate a lot.

They say, "Have you done so-and-so?" They say, "Oh, yes," when actually really miniscule or hardly at all. Conveying straight stories that really tell things the way they were requires a responsibility towards history, which is what I advocate. I've always attempted to do so myself.

But it is important to read and continue to find out what's going on these days. I get *The Wall Street Journal* myself, though I'm not commercializing! Also the *Kiplinger Washington Newsletter*.

CHAPTER EIGHT:
SOME OLD FAVORITES

SOME OF MY FAVORITE ROLES IN MOVIE AND TELEVISION PROJECTS:

Paths of Glory (1957): A WWI military saga of war at its worst.

The Long Hot Summer (1958): I played a difficult role, a Southerner who calls himself "decayed gentry." Money, too much family, etc. I did the opposite: inside I played him like General George S. Patton.

Compulsion (1959): The story of the Loeb-Leopold case.

Six months later, Richard Zanuck (who I later learned saw me in *Long Hot Summer*) called me in for a part in this film which he was about to produce for Fox. He asked me to play a strong part and then he says:

"Tell me about Orson Welles. How's Orson?"

"Oh, he's fine. He stands out there with a book. Right in the hot sun, all day long. And in the morning he has eight boxes of eggs." (True story).

I had some scenes with him and he was starting on his way, but what an actor though. I saw *The Third Man* (1950). Wasn't he something?

Orson Welles made a movie at the age of twenty four which is still voted NUMBER ONE as the finest motion picture ever made: *Citizen Kane* (1941).

The Rifleman (1958–1963): Starring Chuck Connors. Had a string of roles playing gunfighters, gamblers and outlaws. I hear from a lot of people about it.

I went over there once when someone mentioned my name and one of the producers says, "Well, I don't know about him. Bring him in."

With Chuck Connors in *The Rifleman*.
Photo courtesy of Richard Anderson.

He saw that I was tall, so they hired me. I played a guy named Lariat Jones, who was a wanted man. It was a wonderful part. They ended up doing eight of them.

Wanted: Dead or Alive (1958–1961): With Steve McQueen. Had some good scenes with him in his popular Western.

The Gunfight At Dodge City (1959): A gunfighter in a Joel McCrea epic motion picture for the Mirisch brothers. I'd sit there between scenes and listen to him talk about his film career. Great stories with Alfred Hitchcock, Preston Sturges (a great director, one of my favorites, whom I met on *Lights, Camera, Action!*).

Doing various Western characters in *The Big Valley* (1965–1969) starring Barbara Stanwyck and, by the way, I first met up with Lee Majors there.

The Night Strangler (1973): Had a great opportunity in the lead villain role, a two-hour thriller.

The Six Million Dollar Man (1974–1978) and *The Bionic Woman* (1976–1978): I am not leaving out Oscar Goldman! I modeled him after a WWII member of the Roosevelt team. His name was Charles E. Bohlen. An exemplary American behind the scenes of this American victory.

How does Goldman handle these people, both bionic?
Steve Austin: After a mission or two, did not like the set up. HE WANTED OUT.
Lee: We became good friends. Respected each other.
Jamie Summers: *I hate violence, but will get the job done.* There for you Jamie.
Lindsay: You sweet lady…I will be whistling to work for three years!

CHAPTER NINE:
ON BEING AN ACTOR

THE ART AND CRAFT OF ACTING

Someone might ask: What's the beginning of becoming an actor? What might be a good reason for going into the acting business? Here's a good answer: sometimes you can get a good table at a restaurant!

But, seriously, folks. A primary factor in acting is to keep audiences interested in what's going on. For some actors it's part of their genes as the camera loves them—though it may not always be reciprocated! The best example of course is Greta Garbo who famously "vant(ed) to be left alone."

Most of us are not that lucky, so what is seen onscreen is usually a result of our effort to put it there. Once we've done our homework we can step back and let our own "magic" take effect.

In my own case, I am lucky to be very castable. It has been said that I would make "the perfect Internal Revenue Service agent, a hanging judge or the captain of a hell ship." It has been my great ambition to play an American James Bond. With Oscar Goldman and other characters I have been fortunate to have been able to play it somewhere in the middle.

I have often provided the storyline for viewers at the beginning by way of exposition. I set up and send out other characters on some type of suicide mission. That is probably what I am best known for.

Although the character I play is a leader, I try to show some aspects of vulnerability, which is part of any role to one degree or another. With this I try to add humor as I can.

Another part of being an actor is to have as well rounded a life as possible. I enjoy reading and travelling, which helps to broaden my outlook on life and other people.

Physical fitness is important, not just for the physical but emotionally and spiritually too, to relieve stress and improve one's state of mind. Besides tennis as previously mentioned, I've enjoyed skiing, bicycling and swimming.

Perhaps most importantly is to have a personal and social life apart from your work. Many young people have come out to Hollywood to fill some kind of need that has nothing to do with the business itself. We could also list the names of those who have found that out too late, and many more whose names will never be known.

Solitary time adds perspective. I enjoy spending a quiet evening listening to soft piano music while relaxing with a good book An actor needs to explore new opportunities and experiences to draw on but too much social activity can cause one to lose focus.

As I mentioned earlier, when people have asked why I don't write a book about my life, I tell them: I'm still living it!

My agent called one day to say that he wished he had more Richard Andersons: four offers for work that week! Do you know why? No mystery: As the man said: "Learn the lyrics."

"Always be on time, do the homework and don't bump into the furniture." But, most crucially, "Learn the lyrics." The actor who told me that same sentence on the first day of my first motion picture with him at MGM? Spencer Tracy, who I was lucky enough to work with once.

Show up, be on time. That is very, very important because those two things in the film business cost money. And also "Learn the lyrics." Be ready for that, because you never know.

Remember—you are the only one who knows your lines when you go to work in the morning, no one else does. You are going to be delivering the transfer of script to audience. Therefore, that is what your job is, and the way you can do that is to learn the lines so that you don't have to think about them.

It's like a piano: when you play a piece, your fingers remember it, you don't have to think about it when you do it enough. So I cannot emphasize enough, really do your homework. When you come in, you'll feel better. It doesn't mean that you won't be nervous.

It doesn't mean that you wish, as I did, every time I went to work: "What am I doing here? Why am I doing this work? I wish I were a gaffer or an electrician. They come in to work four in the morning, I'll say that for them. They don't have to remember any lines!" They work hard, as I do, but I often sit in a trailer till four or five in the afternoon, without having worked all day.

But I have a speech that's maybe a soliloquy for a page and a half. And the assistant knocks on the door and says "Mr. Anderson, we're ready for you now."

"Oh, fine."

When I get out there, the director says: "Richard, we've got to shoot this now. THE SUN IS GOING DOWN! The sun is going down!

What I am saying is that I have worked with people that do just one take. I say WONDERFUL. I couldn't agree more. And they want to do the first take.

I understand that Clint Eastwood does that. VERY few takes. Angelina Jolie, when she went to work with Clint Eastwood, why he started with practically no rehearsals.

"So let's shoot" and shot it once. "That's fine."

Over here she says "WAIT A MINUTE!" till she got into it.

Doing It His Way

Sinatra did it with most of his recordings. The most extraordinary thing about him is that every song he sings is telling a story. It might be fast, it might be slow but on top of that he can hold a feeling. The way he does it is with his ribs.

He was supposed to play the lead role of Billy Bigelow in the film version of *Carousel* (1956). He was told that he had to shoot his scenes in both conventional 35 millimeter cinemascope and 55 millimeter CinemaScope, for prestigious roadshow screenings.[1]

Although he very much wanted to play the role you know what he did? Quit. Wouldn't do it. Passed on it. He was famously quoted as having only "one good take in me" and that he "signed to do one movie, not two."[2]

That's the way some people work. I don't. I like a lot of takes.

Whatever It Takes

I find out right away what the director is. If he likes takes, I'll take my time. Take your time and build up to it. Now, I hadn't worked with Clint, but if I had worked with him, heck, I'd throw everything in the first time, and that should be enough.

In most cases I agree, that should. That's why his pictures do well for the most part, and come in under budget.

The first scene in the movie is when you want to make sure the director will leave you alone. You really want to give them the "stuff." For example, on the first day of shooting *Curse of the Faceless Man*, I was approached by director Edward L. Cahn. It was in the morning and the other actor, Luis Van Rooten (a wonderful actor by the way) and I were just rehearsing and Cahn looks and asks, somewhat rhetorically, "What are you guys doing?" He was afraid we wouldn't have enough for the take.

Now this guy's used to making quick movies. I mean, he would have been great in television. He said, "Take it easy, you're just rehearsing," and then after the shot he didn't say another word.

But we made it in six days.

What we're doing here is seeing the story of an actor that wasn't afraid to play all kinds of parts. I did outlive the time when a profile was hired to do pictures. They'd seen an actor: "He's good" and they get the picture that's right for him, whereas everybody's doing all kind of different things now.

They think of me that way—which I'm very glad to hear—as that was "the ground I took." They didn't make a star in all the six years I was at MGM except Debbie Reynolds. Nobody broke through. They were too busy trying to keep the place open. The big ones I'm also talking about. Gable even left there.

The fact is, there was nothing to be stuck in because I played everything. One producer was quoted as saying that I didn't have that kind of vulnerability. In other words, you're smart in every way, you know how to do everything. Well, I don't know quite how to answer that other than: Do I have faults? Am I vulnerable?

Absolutely.

By the way, you want to remember, too, that you grow as you go. When things aren't quite perfect, it's not supposed to be, you know.

Don't get hard on yourself, "I could have done that better" which most actors do. As I liked to tell reporters: "I'm just going to keep doing this until I get the bloody thing right."

Which reminds me, in the *Six Million Dollar Man*, producer Harve Bennett came by one day and he asked, "Richard, is it true that you don't watch any of these shows? I heard you just don't watch them."

I said, "No, I don't. I'm just too busy working on two at once and I want to get a little bit of sleep at night."

But in this case we had a good time.

Gregory Peck

I had the opportunity to meet Gregory Peck on occasion. Gregory Peck liked what he was doing, I could see it. He also had a great sense of humor.

I had actually worked for a short time with someone that he had worked with for years, who preferred to remain low-key about her consulting work. Her focus was on really getting a sense of the thoughts of who you were acting against and what the situation is and how you would react to them. I heard about her when I was doing the play *Anna Lucasta*, because the actress who was playing opposite me had gone to her. She had asked me to the rehearsal with her for *Lucasta*. And then I worked with her on and off for a number of years just to get what you call "the thoughts." What are you thinking about when this person is there?

I remember I was watching Gregory Peck in an Elia Kazan movie, *Gentleman's Agreement* (1947), which had to do with anti-semitism. In that scene with the hotel clerk, he was extraordinarily good in the scene by what he didn't do. He took it but you could see it. This is what you work for. He had his big moment. He had a lot of pictures and, not to distract from him, but film acting is 50% face for casting and everything else. They see your face and that's where they get…

Now what you do after that depends on how long you're going to be making pictures. He stayed in a long time. The thing that I object to, strongly, is: just when you think you've really got it, you encounter a thing about age in America.

Gary Cooper was just trying to get work. Gregory Peck would say in the papers, "I'd like to work with Harrison Ford, I'd like..."—meaning he wanted to continue to work. And what he finally was doing, it might have been visually, as he got older or whatever it was, he took sessions at the Los Angeles County Museum of Art and he had readings. He really loved the work, you see, when he really wasn't doing parts anymore. But I assume he WANTED to. Cooper maybe wanted to. So what I'm saying is that maybe they should continue to go on and do that.

The only one that didn't really do that was Cary Grant. He stopped. The last picture he did was in Hong Kong, *Walk, Don't Run* (1964). He said, "I'm not gonna do it anymore." He said, "I want to, for a change, in my life, live in the real world."

LESLIE NIELSEN AND WILLIAM SHATNER

Then there are those actors who take a different path, experiencing whatever comes their way.

Leslie Nielsen, who I had worked with shortly before he passed away, and Bill Shatner are both those kind of guys. Both are Canadian actors, whose professionalism, as I mentioned earlier regarding Raymond Burr, I have come to admire. Leslie played the lead in *Forbidden Planet* and he did a very good job, and he was very straight. Then, as time went on, he suddenly said, "You know, I've got to think of something else."

That's what William Shatner did. He began doing more comedy, which seemed to "take off" you might say, after appearing in the second of the *Airplane* movies. And Bill, golly, it looks like he'll go to the opening of a door! He was singing there for a while, and he's also been nominated for heavy work, of course. Bill just started playing a different game.

I worked with Bill once. He directed an episode of *Kung Fu* titled "Secret Place" in Canada. He was all work. I think basically Shatner is a good guy. He wants it.

And they both figured out what to do. Nielsen just started doing comedy: a klutz! To such a degree that they made movies out of him. And I know people in the East and the Midwest who would just say, "Well, I can't wait till I see those movies," though that ran out of steam. But these people worked. And more than that, it seems they like to work. Or they have to work, or they want to work.

It's amazing. All kinds of different people in this game.

"Learn the lyrics, and don't bump into the furniture."

CHAPTER TEN:
UP CLOSE AND PERSONAL

KATHARINE'S PASSING

In 2004 I had learned that Katharine had been diagnosed with lung cancer, from which she passed away two years later.

They had a reception for her at the big place and everybody came. There were people who didn't like her and so forth…"She was this or that or that…wait a minute!"…you know.

The whole town showed up. They asked me to come and I had to come say good bye.

Her obituary had this to say:

> *"She leaves behind (not only) a grieving family, a good portion of the people in town, who have come to consider her business, Explore Booksellers on Main Street, an extension of their own living rooms. 'I've lived in this valley for 20-plus years,' said one of her competitors, Fred Durham, manager of the Town Center Booksellers in Basalt. 'And for many, many years, Explore Booksellers was like a second home to me.'"*[1]

The whole town showed up. They asked me to come, and I had to come say good bye.

I don't think the girls wanted me to come up the last three weeks. I guess they didn't want me to see her as she was, but we kept in touch.

Then one day she sent a word: it was one word.

She said, "Love."

She died the next day. So I was a very lucky man.

Katharine was the daughter of MGM Producer Irving Thalberg and Norma Shearer, who was one of the biggest film stars of her time. The stresses that resulted from all of this, along with the death of her father at an early age, would leave their mark on her for the rest of her life.

Indian Consortium

I have been working with American Indians in California. I was asked to go to a meeting for what is called the California Indian Manpower Consortium headquartered in Sacramento. They were trying to get education for the current generation and I've been with them ever since, for 23 years. Education is what we were after, to get them out in the workplace. Now they're staying on reservations and starting their own businesses and of course developing educational skills. Really exciting things are happening, too. So they're now developing their own businesses on the reservation. It makes a difference.

Veterans Hospitals.

I have been involved with the Veterans Park Conservancy (VPC) which has worked in partnership with the local and Federal Department of Veterans Affairs (VA) to honor our past, present and future military veterans by the preservation, protection and enhancement of the VA property in West Los Angeles. The VPC was originally formed to protect the property from commercial development and sale.

VPC is currently "developing spaces, amenities and facilities that address veterans' physical, spiritual and mental healing for the estimated 85,000 veterans that live on or access the property."[2]

We have been putting down chain link fences around the cemetery on Wilshire and Sepulveda Boulevards, as well as trees around the graves and a wrought iron gate up for The Soldier's Home. Now we want to put in a park, although we've had to deal with some neighbors that don't want further development along these lines in the area around their homes.

Richard at Veterans Park Conservancy Presentation.
Photo courtesy of Richard Anderson.

We're fighting to get this done, with a budget of seven million dollars.

Fragile X

I do commercials for the Fragile X Foundation which concerns a debilitating disease to newly born babies which, it is said, comes from the mother only and about which not enough is known about. According to the Genetics Home Reference Website: "Fragile X syndrome is a genetic condition that causes a range of developmental problems including learning disabilities and cognitive impairment. Usually, males are more severely affected by this disorder than females" [3]

Those are three active things I'm involved with and I'm called to do other things as well. And between that and involvement with two productions currently in development and conventions, I get out and see what's going on.

Fan Conventions

I'm very heavy into conventions around the world, meeting my fans, where I learn about what people are thinking.

I think the first one was at the Marriott Hotel, it was finally called The Hilton, out by the Burbank Airport in California. They have those there. I went there once. I actually had no idea about it, nor did I necessarily want to do it. I'm doing it because I want to see what it was like. I had to even ask somebody there, "Well, how much do I charge for these pictures?" but I found out I like that, because I meet people from all over the world. I also find out what's going on in this country. Talk to them.

When they come up, some of them look at me the way I looked at Gary Cooper in Mexico City when I first saw him standing there. He looked exactly like he did in the movies. He acted that way and everything else. So they sort of look at me, they don't know what to say about it. So I say, "Where are you from?" and that does it. We start talking. And I'm interested in where they're from.

I have fan clubs. I had one in England and there was one here in the U.S. as well. I still get a lot of stuff from the one in France. They let me know what's playing over there.

Graphic courtesy of Richard Anderson.

THOUGHTS OF EUROPE

Lew Wasserman and Herb Tannen sent me around Europe plugging the *SMDM*.
 Lew OK'd anywhere I wanted to go in the world…during time off from *Six Million Dollar Man*. Only person who was ever given this at Universal…aside from Alfred Hitchcock.
 Stayed at the only great hotel….
 "Hotel du Cap Eden Roc"
 Allowed only certain people…no credit cards…just cash….
 Swam, played tennis…lunch outside with table by the sea.
 Was there a week.

Returned ten years later...swam by the famous rock swimming pool...salt.

The person who took care of it...saw me and shouted:

"Welcome back Mr. Anderson!"

Lew always heard about the actors...were always on time...knew the lines and with a sense of humor.

Tennis Tournaments

I got started with these celebrity tennis tournaments. That's when I saw the world, went around. They were all charity events, for various causes.

Wendall Nyles was the one who organized them. He used to be the announcer for Bob Hope. They were in Europe as well as Singapore. We had wonderful people with us, like

Jonathan Winters. He was really something.

Jack Warner always used to invite me to his house for tennis on Saturday and I had the opportunity to really learn about what these people were like. Karl Malden once said the difference between today and yesterday was these guys were tough guys, no question about it. But if they saw something good, they put more money into it even if it didn't make any money. That would be the comment I would make about them.

The tennis has "served" me well because I learned a lot by meeting new people along the way while doing a lot of charities for Princess Grace in London, Tokyo and France or wherever they were holding events for blind children. It was all tennis.

Once I was invited to a gathering and then afterwards some friends and I decided to take a canal trip the south of France for good times, which is a wonderful place to go. There's a hotel there on the Mediterranean that is always used for the Cannes Film festival. They don't take credit cards. It's the most beautiful hotel I've ever been to,

A Few Regrets

Do I have any regrets? I've had a few...

But to quote the fella who probably sang better than anybody else in the history of singing songs, the fella with impeccable phrasing, rhythm and emotion in his singing: "I've had a few, but too few to mention"—Frank Sinatra.

But this one thing I WILL mention: I didn't take BODY SHOP in high school.

(Readers, I'm talking about automobiles!).

Body shop was a class that you could take where all the guys would go to who were "interested in automobiles, folks." I was always interested in automobiles. I didn't own one at the time. I wish I had gone to Body Shop—to understand and learn—about the incredible invention of the COMBUSTION ENGINE, how it worked and what made it run.

And particularly Fords. To me it was just an extraordinary invention.

I've had such respect for that Henry Ford—he came from a farm and never forgot it. He failed twice or three times before he hit. On a job in Detroit a number of years ago...I was invited to visit the Ford Museum.

The Ford Phaeton

Today I own an old Ford, a 1936 four-door Ford Convertible Phaeton (comes from the word carriages). Any color you want, just as long as its tires are black with white sidewalls!

I found this car in Honolulu, sitting out in front of a shop called Tahitian Imports. I was on my way to shoot a commercial:

...And there it was...The car that I had been dreaming about all my life just sitting there. I asked the ad rep to stop the car. He turned, looked at me and says,

"Mr. Anderson...it's getting...we've got to be there..."

I said "It won't take long...20 minutes" (I prided myself on never being late on a job).

"But..."

I went in, asked for the owner of that car outside. The secretary said, "He's there, go in."

I walked into his office. I said, "That Ford. If I owned it, I wouldn't sell it. But if you ever do, I'd like to buy it. Here's my card."

He says, "Wait a minute, wait a minute, as a matter of fact, I put an ad in the paper that it's for sale. I'm going to buy a '34 Ford."

Before he changed his mind, I said, "I'll buy it"'

He said, "Don't you want to drive it?"'

I said, "No. By the way, how much is it?"

He told me and he also said, "There's no rust in it, I've always kept it up. Everything is original...except I put the battery in the back...runs better."

I agreed to the price...but he says to me, "I won't pay for shipping it over."

I wrote him out a check.

"Before you leave," he said, "I have some advice..."

"Ok with me! Say it quick."

"Since this car is an original, don't do what most people do when they buy a classic car...they spend thousands adding on fixtures. Don't change it, don't make it better, just leave it the way it's built."

I thanked him.

Ten years later, I was back to the Islands shooting *Tora! Tora! Tora!* (1970) and thought I'd slip by to Tahitian Imports to say hello. By God, I saw that '34 Ford in front with all kinds of mirrors, fancy hub caps etc....! He came running out, laughing:

"I didn't listen to my own advice," he said sheepishly.

These days, I often drive it down Sunset Boulevard, west towards the Bel Air Hotel. They all know me, they always want to park the car. Just like the day it was built...no add ons. The top is always down, it's always shining. I polish it myself.

"Driving the Artwork"

Retailer Ralph Lauren had a memorable car show a while back. He owned 30 of the most beautiful cars in the world, including a Bugatti. He made a statement to this effect, which I will always remember:

The Ford Phaeton.
Photo courtesy of Richard Anderson.

People enjoy going to museums to see artwork, or go to galleries. Paintings really do something for people—to see artwork like that is uplifting.

Do you know where Mr. Lauren displayed his cars?

At The Louvre Museum in Paris!

Automobiles, he has stated, have the same effect as pictures in a museum: beautiful to look at, with style and culture.

I'd add to that, "Yes, but with an automobile you can also drive the artwork!"

BROOKE, ASHLEY AND DEVA

I have peace in my life with my three daughters, Ashley, Brooke Dominique, and Deva (that's Sanskrit) Justine Anderson.

My daughters are all amazing in terms of what they wanted to do with their lives. They have exceeded my own expectations for them.

Brooke went to Washington and worked for twenty years with Congressmen and then she had an office in the White House. She then got married, left her life in Washington, and later found a new direction in New York, working at the United Nations and rising to the rank of Associate President.

And then they called her back in the second year. She went back and finally called me one night and said "I've done twenty three years with Congressmen and worked towards nuclear disarmament with the Russians. I just can't anymore, I'm tired."

I said "____ 'em," you know, and she left.

Now she's happily married to one of the fellows she knew in Aspen and now they live in Bosemon, Montana. She has children from her husband's previous marriage who went with Brooke and him, so now they have two children. My daughters never had children, but they all have children now!

Deva heads the music division at Play-Tone, a big music company owned by Tom Hanks and is working in London right now.

Then Ashley has her own public relations firm, which she began in Los Angeles, later relocating to Chicago and then to Aspen. She finally approached me and said "Dad, I don't know where I should live."

I said, "Go back to where you went to college, Santa Barbara." So she's up there. By the way, she's working there in the housing game. Today it's housing and automobiles and she's very much involved there with someone close to her.

People ask me, "How did all this work?" asking questions about how it turned out like this.

I say "Well, I never said anything! They come up and I just stare at my shoes." Like with the Gary Cooper thing.

I brought up my daughters out here, in their early teenage years. I sat them down and told them all I knew in five minutes. Although they always came to me with their problems. Those were years that I really enjoyed them and then they went off to college.

CHAPTER TEN: UP CLOSE AND PERSONAL

With gratitude from the U.S. Air Force, for Richard's work with Veteran's park conservancy.
Photo courtesy of Joint Base Andrews.

PRESENT ACTIVITIES

Of course, I'm often asked if I ever plan to come out of "retirement" for more acting work Although I do substantial voiceover work and receive offers for acting opportunities I'm not really happy with the state of the current films. I'd maybe like to do a kind of older James Bond coming out of retirement type of thing, coming back for just one more mission. (I admire Sean Connery very much).

I guess what I'm trying to say is I'm just starting a whole new life. I think we're very fortunate to live in this country, considering what else is going on in other parts of the world. And that, in my particular happening, I knew what I wanted to do and I've really had an interesting kind of a time with it.

When I go out in my automobile sometimes and stop to see someone, fans will often approach me and say, "There isn't a day that goes by that I don't see you on television!" Every day.

I've always kept a certain sense of humor about it. Because you can't know what else to do!

And I'm saying to myself, I've been very, very lucky. More than lucky. I'm very very in love with the work, with my family, with my old 1936 Ford Convertible.

I am grateful that I was able to pursue the career I always wanted and to have the opportunity to meet Walter Huston, who helped me develop a sense of humor through his words:

"PUT ON A GOOD SHOW AND ALWAYS TRAVEL FIRST CLASS!"

CHAPTER NOTES

"YOU OUGHT TO WRITE A BOOK."

1. *BIONIC WIKI*
http://bionic.wikia.com/wiki/OSI

REAL WORLD

...The closest real-life analogue to the OSI would probably be the extremely short-lived Interim Research and Intelligence Service. This subdivision of the State Department was the result of the devolution of the functionality of the OSS to the Departments of War and State in the immediate aftermath of World War II. By 1946, these functions would be again removed from War and State and reconstituted into the newly-formed CIA. Indeed the fact that the CIA arose out of the efforts of Truman's Secretary of State James Byrnes [6] may also be seen as a possible reason that the fictional OSI is a part of the Department of State. The modern State Department includes the [Bureau of Intelligence and Research], known as INR, but its intelligence gathering activities are not primary covert.

Historically, there was a real Office of Scientific Intelligence that was part of the CIA. On December 31, 1948, the CIA formed the Office of Scientific Intelligence (OSI), by merging the Scientific Branch in the Office of Reports and Estimates with the Nuclear Energy Group of the Office of Special Operations (OSO). In August of 1963, the CIA's Office of Secret Intelligence was transferred into the Directorate of Science and Technology.

A real OSI exists within the Pentagon, although just as in the series, there appears to be a difference of opinion as to what the initials stands for. In 2002, a *New York Times* article referred to an "Office of Strategic Influence,"[7] while others call it the "Office of Strategic Information"[8] (by coincidence this is also one of the names used in the Charlton comic book series). This OSI, which was created after the September 11 attacks, appears to be tasked with disseminating information relating to the War on Terror.

OSI in Other Movies and Literature

The Office of Scientific Investigation is the unifying element of a trilogy of sci-fi movies written by Ivan Tors. The movies include *The Magnetic Monster* (1953), *Riders to the Stars* (1954), and *Gog* (1954). The adventures of the Office of Scientific Investigation in Tors' movies resemble cases that would involve the OSI in *SMDM* and *BW*.

The Office of Secret Intelligence is an organization that plays a prominent role in The Venture Brothers series. The abbreviation OSI is obviously inspired by the *Six Million Dollar Man*. One of its former operatives is Steve Summers, a clear reference to Steve Austin.

The Office of Scientific Intelligence is the name of the government organization in the 1984 film *Firestarter*. In this film, the OSI attempts to control a girl, played by Drew Barrymore, who has the power of pyrokenesis.

The Office of Scientific Intelligence is the name of the government organization involved in combating an alien invasion in the 1994 film *The Puppet Masters*. The film is based on Robert A. Heinlein's 1951 novel of the same name. In the novel, the goverment organization is simply called "Section."

Television

The overwhelmingly dominant name used in televised (and audio) stories is Office of Scientific Intelligence. This was seen on props (like agent identification cards) and sets (such as the outer glass door to Oscar's office) in many episodes, including "Operation Firefly," "The Last Kamikaze," "Return of the Robot Maker," and the "Kill Oscar" trilogy. However, other names have occasionally cropped up.

The single most consistent alternative is Office of Scientific *Information*. This was used throughout the reunion movies. Given the fact that the movies were set several years after the final events of the series, it is possible that the Office of Scientific Intelligence, like many government agencies, got a name change in the intervening years.

Other in-story variations are not so easy to explain, largely because they happened only once and are sandwiched between other stories that revert back to Office of Scientific Intelligence. These are potentially best explained as production errors:

- Office of Scientific Investigation
  ("Welcome Home, Jaime," "Death Probe")

- Office of Strategic Investigation

CHAPTER ONE
RELOCATION

1. Frances B. Carpenter, *The Inner Life of Abraham Lincoln* (Lincoln, Nebraska, University of Nebraska Press, 1995) pp 258-9

CHAPTER TWO
THE MGM YEARS (PART ONE)

1. Stuart S. Nagel, *Ernest Hemingway, The Oak Park Legacy*, University of Alabama Press. (1996) 87
2. A. Scott Berg, *Goldwyn: A Biography*, Penguin Group (USA) Incorporated. (1998) 8-13

CHAPTER FIVE
PERRY MASON, THE NIGHT STRANGLER AND "THE LAST FRAME"

1. Alexa Foreman, email to co-author

Chapter Six
"We Have The Technology"
1. *Dynamite Magazine* #29 "The Man In the Middle—Richard Anderson." November, 1976 pp 4-5
2. *Los Angeles Times* "She's a 21st Century Cyborg" September 26, 2007

Chapter Seven
The Post–"Bionic" Years
1. Knight Kiplinger, email to co-author

Chapter Nine
On Being An Actor
1. Miller Drake, email to author 9/14

In 1955, Mike Todd developed TODD-AO, a 70mm large format film process to compete with the three camera, three projector Cinerama format and the growing popularity of CinemaScope. TODD-AO was a single camera 65mm negative/70mm release print process with a six channel stereo magnetic soundtrack on the film print and an aspect ratio of 2.20. Because TODD-AO was shot at 30 fps (frames per second), supposedly for better resolution, vs. the standard 24 fps speed that was the standard for almost all theaters in the world, it could only play in specially equipped theaters that could project film at 30 fps. This was first used on "Oklahoma," which necessitated shooting a second version simultaneously in 35mm CinemaScope @ 24fps, and also because the ability to make an acceptable 35mm scope reduction negative from the original 65mm negative had not yet been perfected. This is where the "shooting of two versions of the same movie" came in and this is what Frank Sinatra (a famous "first take" actor) was referring too as a reason to bow out of "Carousel." At the time, 20th Century Fox was developing CinemaScope 55 to compete with TODD-AO and were not sure if it would be necessary to shoot two versions of the film as well. As it turned out, they were able to shoot a 55mm large format version of CinemaScope and make high quality 35mm CinemaScope release prints with magnetic stereo

soundtracks. Fox soon dropped the idea of trying to release yet another large film format requiring theaters to install additional projection equipment and released "Carousel" in 35mm CinemaScope only. They shot a second film in CinemaScope 55, "The King And I" which was also released in 35mm CinemaScope and then dropped the process completely. For future 70mm films, Fox would adopt TODD-AO which, after "Around The World In 80 Days," was now changed back to 24 fps for all future productions (with no apparent visual difference), which allowed the movies to be shot once in 70mm for Roadshow engaments and then make a reduction negative for 35mm CinemaScope prints for the regular theaters around the country.
2. Tim Santapietro, *Sinatra in Hollywood*, St Martin's Press. 2008. pp 181-3

CHAPTER TEN
UP CLOSE AND PERSONAL

1. "Katharine Thalberg 1935–2006." *The Aspen Times*. 1/6/2006
2. "About Us." *Veterans Park Conservancy Website*
   http://veteransparkconservancy.org/about.php
3. "Fragile X syndrome." *Genetics Home Reference Website*. Published September 29, 2014
   http://www.ghr.nlm.nih.gov/condition/fragile-x-syndrome

Acknowledgments

Miller Drake—For extensive reviewing, organizational suggestions and moral support.

K. Neil and Susan Earle—For long time interest, encouragement and practical advice.

Alexa Foreman—For her interest and promotional support.

Mandy Horning—Devoted fan and creator of Richard Anderson Fan Club on Facebook, for her passionate interest and promotional support.

Russell Jones—For technical support with graphics.

Scott Mosher—For technical support with formatting.

Ben Ohmart—For his patience, support, interest and humor.

Maria-Christina Pico Verdugo—For valuable contributions and ceaseless dedication.

Don Prokop—My best buddy.—A.D.

All photographs from the Richard Anderson collection.

For more information about Richard Anderson

http://www.bionik.com

Photo courtesy of Richard Anderson.

INDEX

NUMBERS IN **BOLD** INDICATE PHOTOGRAPHS.

Across the Wide Missouri 6, 46-48
Actors Lab, The 33, 34, 36
Adler, Allen 58
Airplane! 126
Alfred Hitchcock Hour, The 55
Altman, Robert 30, 77
Anderson, Ashley (daughter) **80**, 137, 138
Anderson, Brooke Dominique (daughter) **80**, 137, 138
Anderson, Deva (daughter) **80**, 137, 138
Anderson, Henry (father) 9, 12, 33
Anderson, Katharine (wife) 69, 74, 78-80, **80**, 92, 95, 129-130
Anderson, Olga (mother) 9, 33
Anderson, Robert (brother) **10**, 11, 20, 21, 60, 69
Angeli, Pier 55
Anna Lucasta 37, 125
Armstrong, Neil 73
Armstrong, Robert 84
Astaire, Fred 24, 29, 56

Baker, Snowy 39
Balaban, Barney 32
Batman 88
Beaudine, William 88
Bennett, Harve 97, 125

Bergman, Ingrid 22, 35
Big Valley, The 1, 6, 118
Bionic Ever After? 104
Bionic Showdown: The Six Million Dollar Man and the Bionic Woman 104, 105, **105**
Bionic Woman, The 2, 5, 6, 99-104, 106, 107, 114, 118
Block, Irving 58
Blyth, Ann 67
Bohlen, Charles E. 118
Bond, Dennis 73
Boom Town 47
Brokaw, Norman 74
Budge, Donald 18-19
Bullock, Sandra 105, **105**
Burns, Lillian 42
Burr, Raymond 81-85, **82**, 112, 126
Bus Stop 77
Buster Keaton Story, The 67, 69

Cagney, James 76
Cahn, Edward L. 71, 124
Caidin, Martin 7, 95, 105
Camille 24
Camp Roberts 26-28, **26**
Carousel 123, 144-145
"Case of the Positive Negative, The" 83-84

Charlie's Angels 5
Checkmate 77
Cohn, Harry 57
Compulsion 117
Connors, Chuck 117, **118**
Cooper, Gary 7, 11-12, 35-36, 42, 63, 96, 126, 132, 138
Cover Up 111-112
Cowboy and the Lady, The 42
Cozi 107
Crisis 41
Crumpler, Tom 20
Cry in the Night, A 81, **82**, 84
Curse of the Faceless Man 1-2, **4**, 71-74, **72**, 124
Cyborg 7, 95

Dan August 88-89
Darro, Frankie 58
Davies, Marion 28
Davis, Bette 39, 42
Dawn, Jack 91
Day, Robert 112, 113, 114
Disney, Walt 76
Doctor's Wives 6
Donlevy, Brian 83-84
Douglas, Kirk 7, 55, 64, 66
Dozier, William 88
Drake, Betsy 42, 43, **43**, 56, 109
Drake, Miller 73-74
Dream Wife 50
Dr. Strangelove 91
Drydees 103-104
Dynasty 5, 74, 83, 111

Eastwood, Clint 123
Escape From Fort Bravo 2, 6, 50-52

Fawcett, Farrah 99
FBI, The 89
Ferrer, Mel 48

Folsey, George 59
Forbidden Planet 2, 57-60, **58**, 73, 126
Ford, John 39
Ford, Phil 39
Foreman, Alexa 86-87
Forrest, Sally 42
Forsythe, John 77
For Whom the Bell Tolls 35
Francis, Anne 58
Frankenheimer, John 2
Fugitive, The 87, 89

Gable, Clark 2, 6, 7, 24, 31, 35, 46-48, 124
Garbo, Greta 24, 121
Gardner, Ava 24
Gardner, Erle Stanley 85-86
Garfield, John 33
Garland, Judy 56
Gentleman's Agreement 125
Gershler, Abby 74
Goldwyn, Sam 38
Granger, Stewart 2, 43, 48
Grant, Cary 7, 41-43, **43**, 45-46, 50, 54, 56-57, 107, 109, 113, 126
Great Lady Has an Interview, A 56
Green Hornet, The 88
Gunfight At Dodge City, The 118
Gunsmoke 6, 85

Hale, Barbara 84-85
Harris, James 64, 67
Hathaway, Henry 21
Hawks, Howard 45, 46
Hearst, William Randolph 27-28
Hemingway, Ernest 35-36
Hexum, Jon-Erik 111-112
Heyes, Douglas 77
High Noon 35, 96

Index

Hitchcock, Alfred 53-55, 76-77, 118, 133
Hobart, Rose 33
Holden, William 2, 6, 32, 50-52, 84
Hope, Bob 134
Hopper, William 82, 88
Hudson, Rock 89, **90**
Huston, Angelica 30
Huston, John 29, 30
Huston, Walter 28-29, 33, 71, 140

Jackson, Thomas Cornwell 85
Janssen, David 87
Johnson, Kenny 101
Jolie, Angelina 123
Just This Once 53, **53**

Kane and Abel 6
Karloff, Boris 71, 76-77
Kazan, Elia 125
Keaton, Buster 67, 69
Kelly, Gene 24-25
Kelly, Grace 35, 54, 134
Kerr, Deborah 50
Kind Lady 36, **37**
Kiplinger Sr., Austin 112, 113, 114
Kiplinger, Knight 113-114
Kiplinger Washington Newsletter 112-114, 115
Kitten With a Whip 77
Kubrick, Stanley 63-67, 73, 91
Kung Fu 126

Laemmle, Carl 57
Landau, Martin 29
Larson, Glenn 95
Lastfogel, Abe 81
Lawford, Peter 21, 53, **53**
Lee, Bruce 88
Leigh, Janet 53
Levene, Sam 33

Life of Her Own, A 45
Lights, Camera, Action 38-39, 43, 118
Lincoln, Abraham 2, 16-17
Long Hot Summer, The 3, 69-70, **70**, 71, 77, 117
Long Voyage Home, The 34
Lorre, Peter 69
Loy, Myrna 31-32, 38, 47

Macready, George 66
Majors, Lee 95, 96-99, **96**, **98**, 100, 118, 119
Malden, Karl 134
Mama Rosa 40
Manners, David 71
Man of a Thousand Faces 76
March, Fredric 33, 38
Markham, Monte 91
Martin, Quinn 87, 88
Matheson, Richard 90
Mayer, Louis B. 25, 29, 30-32, 38, 49, 50, 57, 69
McCrea, Joel 118
McDowall, Roddy 32-33
McGavin, Darren 90
McGinley, Ted 111
McNamara, Mary 106
McQueen, Steve 118
Menjou, Adolphe 66
MGM (Metro-Goldwyn-Mayer) 2, 5, 11, 21, 23-31, 33, 41, 42, 43, 44-45, 46, 53, 54, 55, 56, 57, 58, 59, 60-61, 63, 64, 67, 69, 86, 91, 122, 124, 130
Miller, Marvin 58
Minnelli, Vincent 2
Monkey Business 45
Monroe, Marilyn 14, 33, 45-46, 77
Montalban, Ricardo 48
Morris, William 71, 74, 81
Mummy, The 71

Murder By Natural Causes 6
"Murder Game, The" 77
Murphy, Francis 26-28
Mystery Science Theatre 3000 77

Nayfak, Nicholas 58
Newman, Paul 7, 69, **70**, 71
New Perry Mason, The 91
New Talent 43
Nielsen, Leslie **58**, 126-127
Night Strangler, The 6, 73, 89-91, 118
North by Northwest 54
Nyles, Wendall 134

O'Brien, Edmond 84
O'Connor, Donald 67
O'Neill, Eugene 34
O'Neill, Jennifer 111

Paley, William 85-86
Pan, Hermes 56
Parker, Eleanor 48
Paths of Glory 1, 63-67, **65**, 73, 103, 117
Patrick, Gail 85
Payment on Demand 39
Pearl 6
Peck, Gregory 37, 66, 88, 113, 125-126
Peg O' My Heart **36**, 37
People Against O'Hara, The 49-50, **49**
Perry Mason 5, 73, 74, 81-87, 88
Perry Mason Returns 112
Phantom of the Opera 76
Pidgeon, Walter 57-58, 64
Playhouse 90 5, 70
Powell, Dick 81
Powell, Jane 24
Powell, William 47
Psycho 76-77

"Purple Room, The" 76-77

Remick, Lee 69
Return of the Six-Million-Dollar Man and the Bionic Woman, The 104
Reynolds, Burt 88-89
Reynolds, Debbie 55, 124
Rifleman, The 1, 2, 6, 117-118, **118**
Ritt, Martin 2, 70

Scaramouche 2, 31, 48
Schary, Dore 42
Schenck, Nick 64
Seconds 2, 89, **90**
"Secret Place" 126
Seven Days in May 2
Shatner, William 126
Shearer, Norma 130
Sheldon, Sidney 53
Sidney, George 31, 48
Sidney, Sylvia 36
Silverman, Fred 99
Simmons, Jean 24, 43
Sinatra, Frank 33, 123, 135, 144
Six Billion Dollar Man, The 106
Six Million Dollar Man, The 2, 5, 7, 29, 73, 86, 95-99, **96**, **98**, 103, 104, 106, 107, 109, 112, 114, 118, 125, 133, 142
Small, Edward 39, 71
Stack, Robert 88
Stanwyck, Barbara 118
Stark, Ray 78
Steiner, Guy 74, 95
Stein, Gertrude 35
Story of Three Loves, The 2, 55
Streep, Meryl 46-47
Strickling, Howard 23
Sturges, John 49-50
Sturges, Preston 39, 83-84, 118

Sun Also Rises, The 36
Sunset Boulevard 32
Swanson, Gloria 32

Talman, William 83
Tannen, Herb 133
Taylor, Elizabeth 24
Taylor, Robert 24, 25, 31
Tempest, The 58
Thalberg, Irving 31, 130
Thaw, Benny 64
Thriller 76-77
Tora! Tora! Tora! 136
Tracy, Spencer 7, 43, 47, 49-50, **49**, 122
Turner Classic Movies 32, 39, 56, 86
Turner, Lana 7, 24, 31, 56
Tuttle, William 91
Twelve O'Clock High 83, 87-88

Untouchables, The 88

Vanishing Westerner, The 39
Van Rooten, Luis 124
Vera-Ellen 24

Wagner, Lindsay 2, 99-104, **101**, **102**, 119

Wahlberg, Mark 106
Walk, Don't Run 126
Wanted: Dead or Alive 118
Warner, Harry 57
Warner, Jack 57, 134
Warner, Sam 57
Wasserman, Lew 133
Webb, Jack 87
Weis, Don 53
Welles, Orson 69-70, 71, 117
Wellman, William 46, 48
Whitmore, James 48
Wilder, Billy 32, 39
Wild, Wild West, The 5
Williams, Esther 47
Williams, Guy 76
Winters, Jonathan 134
Wood, Natalie 7, **82**
Woodward, Joanne 69-70, **70**
Wynn, Keenan 91

Zane Grey Theatre 6
Zanuck, Darryl 57
Zanuck, Richard 117
Ziegfeld Follies 24, 56
Zorro 74, **75**, 76
Zukor, Adolph 57

The Authors

Photo courtesy of Richard Anderson.

Photo courtesy of Alan Doshna.

Foreword by Richard Anderson
www.BearManorMedia.com

CPSIA information can be obtained at www.ICGtesting.com
Printed in the USA
LVOW04*2133050815
448976LV00010B/40/P